To Jenn
Happy Birthday
2003!

THE TEENAGE
INVESTOR

To help you
make your millions

Love
Uncle John
Aunt Celeste
Lecky + Dirk

1 Share
Your Future,
Incorporated

THE TEENAGE INVESTOR

How to Start Early, Invest Often, and Build Wealth

TIMOTHY OLSEN

McGraw-Hill

New York Chicago San Francisco Lisbon London
Madrid Mexico City Milan New Delhi San Juan
Seoul Singapore Sydney Toronto

1 2 3 4 5 6 7 8 9 0 DOC/DOC 0 9 8 7 6 5 4 3

ISBN 0-07-141663-3

Editorial and production services provided by CWL Publishing Enterprises, Inc., Madison, Wisconsin, www.cwlpub.com.

This publication is designed to provide accurate and authoritative information in regard to the subject matter covered. It is sold with the understanding that neither the author nor the publisher is engaged in rendering legal, accounting, or other professional service. If legal advice or other expert assistance is required, the services of a competent professional person should be sought.
    —*From a Declaration of Principles jointly adopted by a Committee of the American Bar Association and a Committee of Publishers*

McGraw-Hill books are available at special quantity discounts to use as premiums and sales promotions, or for use in corporate training programs. For more information, please write to the Director of Special Sales, McGraw-Hill, 2 Penn Plaza, New York, NY 10121-2298. Or contact your local bookstore.

 This book is printed on recycled, acid-free paper containing a minimum of 50% recycled de-inked fiber.

DEDICATION

To my late grandmother,
who truly got me started investing.

Contents

Preface

Some say my age is a positive, others a negative. No matter how it stacks up, I'm 13 years old and dedicated. I'm dedicated to helping novices, especially kids, learn about the subject I love most—investing.

Whether you're investing in stocks, bonds, or mutual funds, there are effective ways to go about it. You'll learn them in this book. You'll learn the best strategies—ways to keep costs down, and ways to diversify in the financial markets. You may be confused by some of the terms in this preface, but you'll soon learn the basics of what you need to know. You'll be on your way to becoming a smart and prudent investor.

The gates open when you learn about accumulating and securing wealth, and I hope my book guides you through that crucial process. It's one thing to become wealthy, but another to stay wealthy—and the people who succeed at staying wealthy are the ones you need to learn from. While you won't be an overnight investment champion, you will learn the basics and then some.

I provide you with case studies, information, factual data, and real-life events that relate to the specific topic I'm discussing in this book. To be a good investor means learning to do your homework, diversifying, and growing and securing your wealth. You'll learn how to do all those things in these chapters.

One of the most important topics covered is *keeping your costs low*. Whether you're investing in stocks, bonds, or mutual funds, it's crucial to keep more of the money working for yourself, rather than giving it away to brokers and other financial advisors.

In my opinion, *you should always pay yourself first*. If you have a job, take some money and either invest it or put it in a bank. You should start a monthly savings plan in a nearby bank so you can have your income work for you. Thanks to compound interest, the money really builds up.

For example, you'll see that if you started at 13 putting $50 into a bank account paying 4% interest every month until you were 16, and then at 16 bumped your monthly deposit up to $75, and then at 20 increased the amount to $300 a month, and then at 40 boosted that monthly figure to $1,000 a month, when you retired at 65, you would have $850,144.31! Just think, you started by setting aside only $50!

At age 13: Put $50 into the bank every month, at 4% interest (for this example).

At age 16: Save $75 a month in same account, for four years.

At age 20: Save $300 per month until age 40.

At age 40: Put $1,000 a month into the same account.

At age 65: You would have more than $850,000!

Naturally, interest rates and the markets will fluctuate, but that's a tremendous return. It requires discipline, of course, but many people can do it. This example proves it's easier to become a multimillionaire than most people think.

Over the course of your investing, you'll learn about investing masterminds, some of whom I profile in this book.

While you may think it's easy to become one of them, I can guarantee you it's not. If you follow their examples and learn something from each of them, you'll eventually have the mindset of an investment expert.

Why Read *My* Book?

Why should you read my book? The answer is simple. If you're young or a beginning investor, I can relate to you. I'm a 13-year-old who's learned a lot about investing since I started at age eight. With this book by your side, you will not have to do any of this alone.

Why will my book help you—maybe more than just about any other investing book? I'm a young investor, I can relate, since I was a beginner not long ago. While I'm not casting any doubt on the credibility of other investment books, mine is different. How many other 13-year-old investors do you know who have been studying the subject since they were eight years old?

One of the keys is that I've learned everything about investing by myself. Of course I've had great mentors and role models, including my family, as well as a few other people who have really made a difference in how I learned to invest. (You can read more about them on the acknowledgments page.)

It's important to learn and follow examples by yourself. I hope this book helps teach you how to be an independent investor, and not be so dependent on other sources for investment ideas. It's always good to get outside input. But remember—it's *your* money.

Do What You Love

Wall Street is in me. I believe there's a piece of it in everyone, whether they know it or not. I get a great feeling talking, reading, or writing about the financial markets. There's a certain magic that surrounds the subject. It's not about the money and it's not about the fame; it's about loving what you do. While I'm no big-shot portfolio manager, I do run my own modest portfolio (with supervision from my parents). And there are few things that I enjoy more.

There are many ways to approach Wall Street and investing, but the fast-paced environment of the investing world will never change. When I visit New York City (in my opinion, the greatest city in the world!), I take time to walk down Wall Street, knowing that, in a few years, I'll be at home there, too.

Goals and Dreams Are a Must

You should also take time to realize that you have goals and dreams. You should be proud of your goals and hold them close to your heart. Dreams and goals are important, because they give you something to work for and something to wake up early in the morning for.

Remember: when you wake up for school or work, it's because you have goals and priorities, and the knowledge and money you'll earn from work is one way to help you achieve your goals. That's why, when asked, I'm never hesitant to talk about my goals.

One day, I hope to be "head of listed trading" for a brokerage or financial firm in New York City. That means that I'll be head of all securities traded on the New York Stock Exchange for my firm. I then hope to start my own business—and treat employees with the amount of respect they deserve, knowing that they're providing for a family or themselves.

I emulate many Wall Street icons, and I hope to be as respected as they are when I get older. I'm not afraid of the future. Instead, I'm rather excited to see what it brings. Good or bad, I know I can make something positive out of it.

When investing, you can make a positive out of every situation, as well—even when your investments don't go as planned. By following the advice in this book, you'll be well on your way to making money investing and achieving your goals and dreams.

Sidebars

I want this book to be practical, to really help kids like me and others to invest wisely and profitably. To assist in achieving that goal and to make the book easy to read, I've included a lot of sidebars throughout. I've broken these sidebars into five different categories, each with its own icon. These are explained just below.

 Sidebars with this icon include applications and examples of the principles you'll read about throughout the book.

 These sidebars provide more explanation about certain topics and give you advice for making good investment decisions.

 The world of investing has its own vocabulary. In sidebars with this icon, you'll find these new terms and concepts defined.

 **Caution**
This icon signals sidebars that give warnings about problems to look out for and mistakes to avoid.

Dollars & Sense
These sidebars provide my tips and ideas for taking advantage of the ideas in the text.

Acknowledgments

I am very grateful to my agent, Sam Fleishman, and my editor, Jeffrey Krames, for their help, encouragement, and belief in me. Thank you to Jeffery for taking a chance on me. Also, thank you to John Woods and Robert Magnan of CWL Publishing Enterprises, Inc. for their invaluable help in editing this book.

I would also like to thank Michael LeBoeuf, Ph.D. Without his mentorship, guidance, and friendship, the book would not have been published.

Many people helped during this process, and their friendship and ideas were invaluable. They include: Richard A. Ferri ,CFA, for looking over and adding his insight to the book, and Seth Tobias, Doug Kass, Paul Silva, Aaron Jacobs, and Larry Swedroe for providing ideas and thoughts on Wall Street.

Of course, the publication of this book would not have been possible without the help from my mom, dad, and sister, Kim, and other family members who provided much needed encouragement.

—Tim Olsen
Cranford, New Jersey

Chapter 1

My Story: The Idea of Investing

I t all started out as an idea. I was so excited about the stock market, and I could not wait to share my newfound interest with everyone I knew. I was young at the time, eight years old, to be exact, and of course I was naïve. Every young person is naïve at one time or another, and I was no exception. It was that summer that my parents introduced my older sister and me to investing in the stock market. I had no idea what investing actually was, and the only resource at my disposal (to the best of my knowledge) was the business television network CNBC.

My dad tried explaining to me what everything meant, but I still had no clue as to what the green, red, blue, and flashing letters meant on the screen. The first stock I bought was PepsiCo (PEP), five shares, when it was trading around $33 a share. My parents told us to buy stock in things we liked.

How I got started investing—and how you can as well.

Of course, these days you must do more research and see how your investment decisions will aid in your overall asset allocation (a subject explained later). My sister chose Disney (DIS). (Little did I know at that age that asset allocation was the principle of one of the greatest mutual fund managers of all time—Peter Lynch of Fidelity Investments.) After I bought the stock, I watched it when I could (usually looking for the updated stock price in the newspaper), just hoping to see the stock price grow to a number greater than $33.

It's Your MONEY **Stock Symbols** Each stock traded on the world's stock exchanges is identified by a symbol. PepsiCo is PEP and Disney is DIS. These symbols are used when stock prices are quoted or reported.

After a year or two, I became *truly* interested in the stock market. I knew I wanted to invest more and I knew that I wanted to make money. But to this day, it isn't the money that drives me—it's the research. I enjoy researching stocks, mutual funds, bonds, and any other type of investment— it's my passion. By watching the financial news shows, I began to understand what the multicolored symbols meant on the screen. I did this to act like I knew something; I think I was the only 10-year-old kid sitting there fascinated by a cable financial news program.

Since that time, I have loved watching the markets through CNBC, the Internet and a variety of other mediums, especially during the summer, while my friends are out playing ball and riding bikes. I remember fondly one show, in the brief few years of the Internet heyday, when CNBC had on the CEO of Juniper Networks—a huge technology company. At the time the stock was trading for more than $300, and it immediately became one of the darlings of the

Internet era, largely because it was fighting fiercely against Cisco Systems (CSCO), another great technology-related success story of the day.

An anchor asked the CEO if the stock could stay at that level or go even higher than $300 a share. The CEO said that he thought that the stock could go higher. As of this writing, the stock is trading for about $10 a share! The CEO was naïve, just like I was—but, as you'll see later in the book, neither the CEO nor I had anything to compare the $300 stock price to. Everyone, I mean *everyone* thought it was OK—and the fact that such companies were making millionaires out of average people made it all the more compelling. There was no comparable benchmark, because Internet and other technology stocks were fairly new, so the price of the stock was justified.

If It Seems Too Good ...
Beware of stock prices that seem too good to be true. They usually are—as we saw in the case of the $300 Internet-era high flyer.

Either way, I knew I could never afford to buy more than one or two shares of such a company, so I continued watching from the sidelines. As it turned out, that was a good choice. A year or two later, the market collapsed. With prices much lower, it was as if most of the stocks were now on sale! So the stock market now looked even more attractive to me, since I could afford some of the stocks that were too expensive in the past. This was a very important lesson for me, as it showed that an excess amount of greed can be hazardous to your wealth. As you'll see in the next chapter, I was determined to turn my ideas into action.

My Story: Turning Ideas into Action

How do you pick stocks to buy? This chapter explains my approach.

As I started getting more interested in investing and finance, I knew I wanted to buy stocks. I consulted with my parents and I began to buy several. I bought stock in a few companies: the first stocks I bought included a cell phone maker and an office equipment company.

How did I choose those companies? I'd just read something that said the stocks would perform well or I liked what the company did. I didn't really do any in-depth research. In the end, I ended up selling those stocks for a loss about a year later. Why? I think it was largely because I hadn't done my research. I decided then that there was simply no way to get ahead in the markets without doing my "homework," and this goes for all types of investments.

I'm proud to say today that, aside from help from mentors and my family members, I've taught

Look Before You Leap There are few shortcuts in investing. It doesn't make sense—and certainly not dollars—to jump into buying a stock. I recommend extensively researching companies and stocks before deciding to buy them.

myself much of what I know. I'm very proud of that fact and that I have learned how to properly research almost any type of investment. (And you'll learn how to do this too, in later chapters.)

Back when I started investing and was determined to buy more stocks, I bought them by researching what they did and by researching some of their *financials* and other facts and figures that could make a difference on the stock price. I then bought a few more stocks based on the principle that I could make money by doing my research.

Term **Financials** Financials is a quick way of referring to financial statements and other reports that present the financial status of a company. Financials include annual and quarterly balance sheets and income statements, annual cash flow statements, and annual ratios.

Do Your Homework!

At that time I was eleven. It was about then that I noticed something meaningful—the stocks I researched had something, a positive catalyst, in other words, something that sparks the stock to do well. The stocks that lagged were the ones I did hardly any research on, and were usually in some sort of trouble financially or had just done something to cause the stock price to go down.

Needless to say, I became hooked—and a "research maven." I researched stocks by reading things on the Internet and in books, magazines, newspapers, etc. One important factor to mention: I never took any of the advice offered by newsletter and magazine writers, though many times it was tempting. After all, the thought of capitalizing on other people's work is very enticing. Instead, I used their conclusions to aid my own work. I now read economic reports from the Federal Reserve and research firms, academic studies, risk analysis research, and a variety of other tools that will help me select stocks or other investments for my asset allocation. In the end, I did capitalize on my own research, and some of the research of analysts and market observers and I'm proud to say I did. While other kids were watching television and playing computer games, I was hooked, researching various types of investments.

 **Think for Yourself** Don't blindly follow the advice of newsletters and other so-called experts. Ignore stock tips and rely on your own informed judgment.

So, what gave me my head start? One of the most influential books I read when I was younger was a book by legendary mutual fund manager, Peter Lynch, titled *Beating the Street*. Now, looking back a few years later, I've realized that other things have helped me along the way, as well. I began to follow many of the principles and ideas of John Bogle, the legendary founder of the Vanguard Group. Another crucial role model for me was, and still is, Berkshire Hathaway's leader, Warren Buffett. The investing principles of these titans all aided in my research of various types of investments—Peter Lynch in stocks, John Bogle in mutual funds, and Warren Buffett in value stocks and whole companies.

While I was researching, I continued to buy stocks. Now, I've become very adept in my research of stocks, mutual funds, and bonds by reading lengthy academic papers, research findings, and SEC filings and listening to company conference calls. Of course I don't stop there; my process becomes much more involved.

I occasionally send e-mails to the managers of companies for clarification on a particular question or point I may have. Most of the time I get a response (especially if it's a smaller company with fewer employees where the management's e-mail addresses are actually on the company's Web site). All of these factors aid in my research and, as you'll see in a later chapter, also help in selecting companies to invest in. (I'll guide you through my process on how to select specific companies later.)

There's no get-rich-quick scheme or the like behind it; instead, so much of investing comes down to good, solid research. I'm not saying research will pay off for you all of the time; my track record has not been perfect. (Nobody's is.) But when you do research, chances are your losses will be minimized.

However, there's one note of caution I should mention here. There is a theory called the *efficient market hypothesis* (or *efficient market theory*) that basically says that all the information that is out there is already reflected in the price of a stock. This means that as soon as news of some sort is announced by a company or if an analyst changes his or her rating on the stock, it will be

Efficient Market Hypothesis

This theory, which evolved in the 1960s, states that in an active market in which many investors are well-informed and intelligent, the prices of securities will reflect all available information. In other words, there are enough smart people buying and selling that the prices they offer and accept will be appropriate. So, if a market is efficient, you can't expect any information or analysis to give you an edge.

immediately reflected in the stock price because of how rapidly shares trade and how quickly many institutional investors act upon the information. There is some-thing to this, but my own experience is that there's simply no excuse for not doing all of the necessary legwork.

If you research—rather than guess—when buying stocks, your odds of making money greatly increase. I hope you learn a lot about the markets and educate yourself, just like I did. If I can do it, you can too!

An Introduction to Financial Markets

W hile many Americans consider markets only within the United States, there are hundreds of financial markets that span the globe—*stock, bond, options,* and *futures* markets (which I'll explain later). All of them provide a structure to our world's economic system. That system is based on cash—not just the U.S. dollar, but also hundreds of other currencies in other countries around the world.

The reason that the U.S. stock markets are the most talked about in global media is because the U.S. is such a world superpower, both economically and militarily. However, there are markets all over the world, and I'll begin to explain how the major world financial markets work and how they can help make you money.

N ow we're going to really get into it—stocks, bonds, and more and how you can begin to make sense of it all.

The Stock Market

The stock market within the United States is huge, in part because the U.S. is one of the most economically powerful countries in the world. A stock market is just that—a place where stocks are bought and sold. The stocks are listed on *exchanges*, such as the NYSE (New York Stock Exchange), the AMEX (American Stock Exchange), and the NASDAQ (National Association of Securities Dealers Automated Quotation System), which are three exchanges based in New York City.

All of the exchanges within the U.S. make up the United States stock market. All of the exchanges in Canada—such as the Toronto Stock Exchange, the Montreal Exchange, and the Vancouver Stock Exchange—make up the Canadian stock market. The same goes for every other country in the world that has at least one stock market. Perhaps you've heard of the London Stock Exchange in England or the Tokyo Stock Exchange, as well.

There are two types of stocks listed on an exchange: *common* and *preferred*. Whenever you hear about stocks in an investment program, chances are it's a common stock. But whether the stock is common or preferred, it's a piece of a company, known as *equity ownership*. Equity ownership simply means you have an ownership interest in the company. There are several differences between common and preferred stock.

By owning a common stock, you're entitled to vote on issues that pertain to the company and are also entitled to make money from the stock by way of *dividends* and *capital appreciation*.

Dividends are money paid out to shareholders that is not going to be reinvested in the business. Established

Dividend A dividend is a periodic payment (usually quarterly) made by a corporation to its shareholders, at the discretion of the board of directors. Dividends represent earnings that the corporation does not reinvest. Some stocks pay no dividends; others pay substantial dividends. Dividends are usually taxable in the year that the shareholders receive them.

companies are most likely to pay out dividends, while many smaller companies don't have the capital to do so.

Capital appreciation occurs simply when the price of the stock rises. For example, if you buy one share of stock at $5, and it rises to $10, your capital appreciation or capital gain is $5. However, you realize (get) the gain only if you sell your one share at $10. If you choose to hold it and it goes to $20, your capital gain or appreciation would be $15. However, if the stock falls back to $5 and then you sell, your capital gain is zero.

Capital appreciation Capital appreciation is an increase in the market price of an asset. With stocks, it's the difference between the amount paid when buying shares and the amount received when selling them.

Preferred stock, on the other hand, entitles shareholders to receive dividends *before* the shareholders with common stock receive them. In the event a company goes bankrupt or liquidates, bondholders and preferred stockholders get paid before the common stockholders (assuming there are funds to be paid out!). However, preferred stock shareholders do not get voting rights like common stockholders.

So, which is better—common stock or preferred stock? The answer to that question depends on your situation and your goals. There are advantages and disadvantages to each, but they should be judged only in terms of your goals and how each type of stock would work for you.

Stock Indexes

An index is a group of stocks selected according to a certain criterion, to represent a specific portion of the market, an industry, or an asset class. An index gives investors like you a quick, overall picture of the performance of the market in general or of a certain industry or of certain sizes or types of companies. In a way, it's like surveying 100 or 200 or 500 people to get an idea of what 250 million people are thinking. Believe me, since there are more than 5,000 stocks traded on U.S. exchanges, it's a lot easier to understand the big picture through indexes than to look at all the small print and get lost in it!

 **Index** An index is a group of stocks selected according to a certain criterion, to represent a specific portion of the market, an industry, or an asset class. The purpose of an index is to give a quick, overall picture of performance. Investors use these composites to measure the overall health of specific markets and as benchmarks of comparison.

In addition to giving you an easy way to track the performance of the market or specific sections of it, an index can serve as a benchmark, a way to judge how a specific stock is doing compared with the stocks of similar companies.

In the next few pages, I'll outline the most important indexes.

Dow Jones Industrial Average (DJIA)

Many people hear about the Dow Jones Industrial Average (DJIA), a stock index, and wrongly label it "the stock market." That's because, when you catch the 30-second financial news segment on the radio or TV, when they mention that the market is up or down, they generally mention how the Dow Jones Industrial Average closed.

But "the Dow," as many investors call it, is in no way, shape, or form "the stock market." The Dow is an index made up of 30 blue-chip companies. When the Dow was unveiled by Charles Dow—founder of Dow Jones and *The Wall Street Journal*—on May 26, 1896, there were only 11 stocks, mostly established, blue-chip railroad companies.

Blue chip A blue chip generally refers to the stock of a large, established company. These companies are considered a safer, more solid investment, because they are less risky.

The DJIA is maintained by the editors of *The Wall Street Journal* and the list is changed only occasionally (www.djindexes.com). As of this writing, the DJIA consists of these 30 stocks:

Alcoa (AA)	Honeywell (HON)
American Express (AXP)	IBM (IBM)
AT&T (T)	Intel (INTC)
Boeing (BA)	International Paper (IP)
Caterpillar (CAT)	Johnson & Johnson (JNJ)
Citigroup (C)	J.P. Morgan Chase (JPM)
Coca-Cola (KO)	McDonald's (MCD)
Disney (DIS)	Merck (MRK)
DuPont (DD)	Microsoft (MSFT)
Eastman Kodak (EK)	Philip Morris (MO)
Exxon Mobil (XOM)	Proctor & Gamble (PG)
General Electric (GE)	SBC Communications (SBC)
General Motors (GM)	3M (MMM)
Hewlett-Packard (HPQ)	United Technologies (UTX)
Home Depot (HD)	Wal-Mart (WMT)

Many Wall Street experts do not like the idea of the DJIA being an indicator of the market as a whole, considering there are only 30 stocks in the average. This subject has been debated many times in academic and professional research reports. Personally, I consider the Standard &

Poor's 500 (S&P 500) a more appropriate indicator of the U.S. stock market's overall strength or weakness. Since there are 500 stocks in this index, it represents much more of the whole stock market than an index that has only 30 stocks.

Still, the Dow is the most commonly referenced and most closely followed stock index. On CNBC, it appears at the top of the index list on the right side of the screen; on most other cable news shows, it appears at the bottom. On the MSN Money Web site, moneycentral.msn.com, it's in the upper right of the screen. In fact, you can find it virtually wherever you find stock market quotations. It differs wherever you get your information.

One reason the index is so widely followed is because it's been around for so long. For more than 100 years it's been the index that has been recognized for following some of America's bluest blue chips, giant firms that shaped the way Americans do business.

The decision to add or remove a stock from the Dow Jones average is the choice of the editors of The Wall Street Journal. In almost all cases, a stock is added or taken out only if a listed company is acquired by another company, a listed company files for bankruptcy, or something of that nature.

Standard & Poor's 500, 400, 600

Perhaps a more fitting index that tracks the market as a whole is the Standard & Poor's 500, more commonly known as the S&P 500 or even just S&P. The S&P 500 (www.standardandpoors.com) includes 500 of the largest stocks by *market capitalization*. The S&P 500 is usually quoted with the DJIA and the NASDAQ Composite on most of the cable TV news shows. The S&P 500, as many academics suggest, is more fitting to represent the broad market.

"The S&P 500 is a basket of 500 stocks considered to be widely held," according to Investor-Words.com. The S&P 500 is weighted by market value. To come up with the value of the S&P 500, all of the stock prices in the index are added up and then divided by 500. It's as simple as that.

Standard & Poor's (part of McGraw-Hill, the company that publishes this book) has two other indexes—the S&P 400 and the S&P 600. They are similar to the S&P 500, except that the S&P 400 tracks 400 mid-cap stocks and the S&P 600 tracks 600 small-cap stocks. The 400 and 600 aren't widely followed by financial news programs, but the Street (Wall Street, of course!) takes note of the performance of each and every index, as it's essential to see how each class of stock is performing relative to the broader market. Certain investment firms put out investment products known as *exchange-traded funds.* I'll cover these in Chapter 7; at this point, it's enough for you to know that an exchange-traded fund is a fund that tracks an index, but can be traded like a stock. These funds can follow the S&P Mid-Cap 400 Index and the S&P Small-Cap 600 Index. One such fund that tracks the S&P Mid-Cap 400 Index is the iShares S&P MidCap 400 Index (IJH). It is an exchange-traded fund put out by Barclays Global, a large U.K.-based financial services firm. There's also an exchange-traded fund that tracks the S&P Small-Cap 600 Index, called the iShares S&P

SmallCap 600 Index (IJR). Both funds can be bought and sold like stocks throughout the trading day on the American Stock Exchange (AMEX).

Wilshire 5000 Equity Index

The Wilshire 5000 Equity Index is a market value-weighted index, just like the S&P 500. The Wilshire 5000 tracks all stocks traded on the New York Stock Exchange and the American Stock Exchange and many of the more active over-the-counter (OTC) stocks. Over-the-counter stocks include shares traded on the NASDAQ.

The Wilshire 5000 is a product of Wilshire Associates, which also created the Wilshire 4500 Index, in 1983, by removing the 500 stocks in the S&P 500 from the Wilshire 5000. You can find more information on the Wilshire indexes on their Web site, wilshire.com.

New York Stock Exchange (NYSE) The New York Stock Exchange is the older and larger of the two major, traditional stock exchanges. Founded in 1792 and located at 18 Broad Street in New York City since 1903, it's where the stocks of about 2,800 companies are traded.

American Stock Exchange (AMEX) The American Stock Exchange is the younger and smaller of the two major, traditional stock exchanges. Located at 86 Trinity Place in New York City, it's home to about 850 stocks.

NASDAQ NASDAQ (Nasdaq) is an electronic stock exchange network run by the National Association of Securities Dealers (NASD). NASDAQ stocks are listed and traded electronically, rather than on the floor as in a physical exchange like the NYSE and the AMEX.

Over-the-counter (OTC) stocks OTC stocks are traded through dealers across the U.S. linked together by telephones and computers. OTC stocks tend to be newer, smaller, and riskier than stocks listed on exchanges and with OTC trading it's much harder for investors to be sure of paying or getting a fair price.

Russell 1000, 2000, 3000

The Frank Russell Company, a consulting firm based in Tacoma, Washington, produces a family of 21 U.S. equity indexes (www.russell.com). You should know about three of them. The *Russell* 3000 is an index of the 3,000 largest U.S. companies, based on total market capitalization; it represents about 98% of the investable U.S. equity market. The *Russell* 1000 consists of the 1,000 largest companies in the Russell 3000. The *Russell* 2000, as you're probably guessing, is an index of the remaining 2,000 companies from the Russell 3000. It's as easy as 1, 2, 3!

Other Indexes

There are various other indexes that track all types of markets and stocks and even specific industries such as oil, consumer products, aerospace, defense, etc. As you'll see later in the book, *index investing* is an efficient and somewhat carefree way to build wealth over time. Index investing is the process of buying groups of stocks, often in mutual funds that own stocks in a particular index, such as the S&P 500. As I'll discuss later, you can invest in index mutual funds or exchange-traded funds (ETFs) and either way you'll be tracking an index or an appropriate benchmark, rather than buying individual securities.

The Basket Method

Index investing—or buying baskets of stocks—is one of the best ways to build wealth over the long run.

Morningstar and the Vanguard Group have listed the larger stock indexes in the following table.

Index	Description
Wilshire 5000	total domestic stock market
S&P 500	large-cap stocks
Wilshire 4500	medium- and small-cap stocks
Russell 2000	small-cap stocks
MSCI EAFE	major foreign stocks
MSCI Europe	major European stocks
MSCI Pacific	developed Australian, Japanese, and Far Eastern stocks
MSCI Emerging Markets	foreign stocks other than developed markets

The Bond Market

The bond market is also a financial market, but not like the stock market. When you buy a stock, you own a piece of that company (*equity ownership*). But when you invest in the corporate bond market, you buy the debt of a company. In other words, you're lending the company money, which the company usually uses to finance a project or to put to work as *working capital*. For lending them money, they pay you a fixed interest rate.

Just as there are various types of stocks, there are various types of bonds. They range from bonds as safe as T-Notes (Treasury Notes), backed by the U.S. government, to *junk bonds* (also known as *high-yield bonds*), which is the debt of a distressed company. Rating agencies such as Standard & Poor's, Moody'sI nvestors Service, and Fitch Ratings rate bonds based on the financials of the companies issuing those bonds. If the financials are terrible, the rating agencies might

 **Junk bonds** Also known as *high-yield bonds,* junk bonds are bonds issued by organizations that are not rated as investment grade by one of the credit rating agencies, because of a risk of default.

Less Risk, But Not No Risk

Bonds are usually considered less risky investments than stocks. Keep in mind, though, that bonds differ in type, interest rates, and risks. Know the rating of any bond that you're considering for your portfolio.

give a company's bond a rating below *investment grade*, meaning that the debt of a company is substantially more risky than that of a well-established corporation.

Traditionally, many investors consider bonds as a safe haven and move into them when the stock market and the economy take a turn for the worse. Investors look to bonds to provide a steady rate of income in uncertain markets, as well as to diversify their portfolios.

Diversifying means buying various investments in order to spread the risk among a number of different investments. Diversification is very important, particularly when markets are not doing well. Since bonds are considered safer than most stocks, they tend to

Diversification

Diversification is dividing investment funds among various investments in order to minimize the risk.

lower the risk of your investments as a whole. In Chapter 5 you'll see how bonds work and what investors use them for.

You can invest in bonds by purchasing individual bonds or through bond mutual funds. Both approaches have their advocates, but bond funds are more convenient and usually better if you're investing less than $50,000.

Morningstar and the Vanguard Group have listed the larger bond indexes in the table.

It's Your MONEY

Buy Bonds

Buying bonds or bond funds is one of the best ways to reduce the risk of your investment portfolio.

Index	Description
Lehman Brothers U.S. Aggregate Bond	total domestic taxable fixed income issues (not including junk bond issues)
Lehman Brothers Government Bond	total U.S. Treasury issues
Custom indexes	as required

Where Do I Start?

A lot of people want to invest, but unfortunately, not many know where to begin. The first and best way is by saving money. Before you invest, you need to put money aside, specifically into a bank account that pays interest or an account set up with an investment firm. Whether it's 1% or 5%, you need to put your money into a savings account, so while you're deciding how and where to invest according to your goals, your principal will be gaining interest. Consider the following example.

You start with $1,000 in a bank account paying you 2.5% interest. If you keep your money in the bank for one year, with 2.5% interest paid out every month, and then add $100 to it every month, you'll have $2,239.13 in one year. That's not bad for one year of deciding how you want to go about investing your money. While the one-year profit may not seem like much, it's not bad because your objective wasn't to make money from that. You were waiting and deciding on what you should be doing with your money. The longer you keep your money in that account, the more it adds up.

What if you decide to plunge into the financial markets? Where should you start? If you're young, always remember that time is your most precious asset. Once it's gone, you can't get it back. The longer your time horizon, the more time you have to make money.

Let's assume that you finally decide you want to invest in stocks. You've realized that you have a long time horizon, say 50 years, and you think you'll make money over the long term investing in stocks. One way to invest might be to put most of your money into an index fund, such as the Vanguard 500 Fund or any other index fund that owns the stocks in the S&P 500, and a smaller percentage into stocks. If you're not sure which stocks to buy or you want to reduce your risk even more, you can just invest in a low-cost index mutual fund. (This is what John Bogle, the legendary founder of Vanguard, recommends.)

If you have a long time horizon, however, you may want to start out investing in a somewhat more aggressive index fund, one that has low expenses and that has the potential to offer substantially larger returns. As for stocks, with so many to choose from (there are thousands listed in the major exchanges in the U.S. alone), it's only natural that you may not know which ones to buy. It is usually best to buy stocks in both large and small companies. Small companies may have greater growth prospects, but the larger companies may have a pattern of consistent earnings growth.

In later chapters, you'll learn which stocks will fit your needs and how to go about researching them, if you're looking to invest in stocks. The other chapters in this book will help you learn more about stocks, bonds, and mutual funds and how you should go about investing in them in a manner that best fits your goals.

Risk in the Financial Markets

Whether you're investing in stocks or bonds, both carry certain risks. Bonds are usually safer than stocks. Stocks and

higher-yielding bonds can be tremendously risky. It's important to understand that the greater the risk, the greater the potential reward. The less risk you choose to take, the less reward. It's as simple as that. Also, as mentioned earlier, the most important thing to understand is that you need to diversify your portfolio over several types of investments.

Buying individual stocks and other more speculative investments is a tremendously risky way to go about investing. In fact, first-time investors would be well-advised to avoid investments like junk bonds altogether, understanding that the risk is simply too much.

One of the greatest risks posed by the stock market can be that of investing in smaller, lesser known companies. Some examples of small companies are U.S. Plastic Lumber (USPL), Coeur d'Alene Mines (CDE), and Emerson Radio (MSN). Generally speaking, the smaller the company, the riskier the investment. It's generally less risky investing in larger, more established companies, such as Microsoft (MSFT), PepsiCo (PEP), and General Electric (GE).

It's possible to make money on any type of stock, whether the company is small, medium, or large. Remember: any type of investment you make always has some sort of risk involved. If there were no risk, you would never be able to gain a return on your investment.

Foreign Financial Markets

The United States has one of the most developed and safest monetary systems in the world; as such, it's traditionally the best place to invest. Some foreign financial markets are exceptionally riskier. At times, the U.S. markets can fall out of favor and investors may want to look to other countries throughout the world for better returns on their investment. Therefore, it's best to look not only at the U.S. markets for investment opportunities, but also at the opportunities in other countries.

There are three types of classifications for investment within specific countries. You can invest in *developed* countries like the United States and Japan. You can also invest in *emerging* markets, which are in a phase of rapid growth, economically and politically. But, with the obvious chance for greater reward, it carries a significant and equal amount of risk. The third category consists of countries with no financial markets; you would have to take steps to invest in private companies with that country, therefore taking substantial risk.

By choosing to invest in foreign markets rather than domestic (U.S.) markets, you may be exposing yourself to significantly more amounts of risk. That's why

Markets Emerging

An emerging market is a country working to improve its economy and rise to the level of the world's more advanced nations. Among the countries considered as emerging markets at this time are Argentina, Brazil, China, Czech Republic, India, Indonesia, Mexico, Peru, Poland, Russia, South Africa, South Korea, and Turkey.

I do not recommend that first-time investors turn to international markets right away. But if you decide to invest abroad, the best way to curb risk is to diversify among all types of countries, so you will be prepared in case one or a few of them face economic and/or political turmoil.

Financial Markets: Summary

The concepts described within this first chapter are just the beginning of what you'll learn throughout the rest of the book. I'll discuss many of the concepts I discussed in this chapter, but in more depth. If you're a novice, don't worry: you have a lot to learn, but the rest of the chapters in this book will help you in your quest to achieve your investment goals. For now, you should keep in mind the key points in this chapter:

- There are many types of financial markets: stock, bond, futures, and options. (There will be more on these later in the book.)
- There are two types of stocks—common and preferred—and both represent equity ownership of a company.
- There are indexes for both stocks and bonds, and an investor can buy the index via the index fund—a helpful and important investment vehicle discussed in depth later in the book.
- There are different types of bonds and the interest rates vary between them, but so do the risk/return ratios: what you get is not always what you pay for.
- Foreign financial markets, specifically emerging markets, are significantly riskier than those of the United States.

Chapter 4

The Wealth Plan for Young Investors

I f you're an investor who's just starting out, this chapter will help you get started. The Wealth Plan for Young Investors is a simple, no-nonsense plan that will help you achieve your goals with a minimum of risk. It does not involve investing in stocks (although you can do that on the side). Instead, it recommends putting your money in savings accounts for varying amounts of time, based on your time horizon.

As you'll see below, the Wealth Plan for Young Investors is a basic and somewhat easy way to manage and create wealth. Though it's designated as "the Wealth Plan for Young Investors," it can also be used by anyone hoping to produce some income (although it usually "creates" more wealth for younger investors).

My thoughts on how you can get started as a young investor.

The Wealth Plan for Young Investors: Step 1

The first and most important step in the wealth plan is to write down your goals and time horizons on a piece of paper. For example, if you're 18, then you might consider your time horizon from age 18 to whatever ending year you think is appropriate. Usually the ending age is the year you wish to retire or when something significant is going to happen in your life, such as buying a house, getting married, starting a family.... The reason this is Step 1 is because you've got to know where you're going and when you expect to be there in order to know which investment vehicles are most likely to get you there. Once you know your time horizon, we can proceed to Step 2.

The Wealth Plan for Young Investors: Step 2

Step 2 involves choosing your bank. One that's close to home is most likely your best bet. In making your selection, you should check to see if the bank offers a savings account for young people. For example, in my area, there's a bank that offers young people up to 18 years old an account paying an interest rate higher than regular savings accounts for adults.At that bank, if you open up an account and deposit money, you'll receive $10, which is then deposited into your account. Why do banks pay kids a higher interest rate? They do this to encourage young people to start saving early, a very important part of financial success. Before you open up an account you need to make sure you understand the types of accounts you can open. You usually have a few choices. So let's explore these.

Certificates of Deposit (CDs)

A CD is a savings account that typically pays an interest rate higher than the bank's regular savings account. The primary reason is because of the requirements of a CD account. When you put your money into a CD, you do it for a certain period of time. Then you can't take it out during that time or you have to pay a penalty, which is usually only interest that was paid to you. Rarely (if ever) will a bank take away your principal from you. For example, on a 30-day CD, some banks will charge you all of the interest you gained as a penalty for withdrawing before the 30 days is up. That restriction is the trade-off for receiving a higher interest rate.

Certificate of deposit (CD) A certificate of deposit is a savings account for a set period of time. It typically offers a higher interest rate than regular savings accounts but there's a penalty if you withdraw the money before the term ends.

The longer you tie up your money, the higher the rate. The typical durations of CDs are three or six months and one, two, three, or five years. There are even CDs that have shorter durations, such as 30 days! There's usually a minimum amount you have to deposit for a CD, often $500 or more, but that amount varies.

There's no risk of losing your money when you put it into a CD, since it's insured by the Federal Deposit Insurance Corporation (FDIC). This means that if the bank goes broke, your deposit is insured by the U.S. government up to $100,000.

There are two main types of CDs, *income* and *growth*.

An income CD pays interest monthly. This is good for people who want to supplement their incomes, such as people who are on fixed incomes. But in order for the monthly

The FDIC

The Federal Deposit Insurance Corporation is a government agency responsible for maintaining the stability of the nation's financial system and sustaining public confidence in the system. The FDIC was created in 1933 to insure deposits and promote safe and sound banking practices.

check to be worth cashing, you have to invest a big chunk of money in the CD, such as $25,000 or more. In fact, many banks don't even offer income CDs for less than $10,000. Since the interest does not remain in the account to accumulate, your annual percentage yield (APY) is the same as your interest rate.

A better choice is a growth CD: the monthly interest remains in your account and earns interest. Because of that compounding (we'll discuss this factor later in this chapter), growth CDs offer a higher APY, which makes them a wiser investment option for people who want to make money over a long term.

Term **Annual percentage yield (APY)** The annual percentage yield is the effective annual rate of return, based on the interest rate and compounding for one year. For example, if the periodic rate is 1% per month, the APY is 12.68%. Truth in Savings regulations require financial institutions to disclose the APY on interest-bearing deposit accounts.

There's a type of CD that's aimed at younger investors with less money and people who may need to access their money in case of an emergency. These may be called *flexible* CDs or *flex* CDs or by such names as *no-penalty, bump-up,* or *liquid.* Check around and ask questions. Find a CD that fits your needs and your budget. As you would expect, flexible CDs usually offer a lower interest rate because of the flexibility they allow.

I recommend putting your money into a CD with a

somewhat longer duration, such as one year, which makes sense for younger investors. Some people may think a five-year CD would be OK for younger investors, but the reality is that if you're 14 or 15, five years later you would be 19 or 20—just about the time when you'll start needing money for larger, more expensive things. Also, if you ever needed to take it out earlier (which is most likely what would happen), you'd be forced to pay a large penalty. In this case, a one-year CD makes a lot more sense for younger investors.

Money Market Accounts

A money market, aka *money market deposit account* and *money market demand account* or *money market savings account*, is an account available at many banks, credit unions, and savings and loan associations. Unlike CDs, money market accounts are liquid: you can usually write several checks against the account per month. They are also safe, because they're insured by the FDIC. And they're stable, because they invest only in debt instruments with maturities of a year or less. Unfortunately, you pay for the liquidity, safety, and stability: interest rates on money-market accounts are low, so you might not even be able to keep up with the rate of inflation. However, these accounts can be a convenient place to store money that's "between investments."

Money market account A money market account is a liquid, interest-bearing account that allows limited transactions. The interest is based on short-term interest rates. Money market accounts are available at many banks, credit unions, and savings and loan associations. It's also known as a *money market deposit account,* a *money market demand account,* and a *money market savings account.*

Money Market Funds

A money market fund is an account that's managed by a firm that invests in *commercial paper* and *treasury market securities.* The account is typically very safe, but—unlike the CD and the money market account—it's not insured by the FDIC. That means if the firm that's managing your account goes bankrupt, you'll most likely lose all your money in that account. (This very seldom happens, by the way.) A money market fund, on the other hand, shares many of the characteristics of a checking account and a money market account. Although the money market fund is not insured by the FDIC, it's usually offered by a bank or brokerage firm, it's highly liquid, but it usually has a lower interest rate than most other investments.

Money market funds, like CDs, typically pay a slightly higher interest rate than an average savings account, but the rate (like all accounts) fluctuates. I recommend that people

Money market fund A money market fund is a type of mutual fund that invests in short-term securities, such as commercial paper, government securities, certificates of deposit, and other highly liquid and safe securities. Money market funds are not federally insured, although the portfolio may consist of guaranteed securities and/or the fund may have private insurance to protect investors.

Commercial paper Commercial paper is the term for unsecured short-term promissory notes that companies issue to obtain cash. Commercial paper is a fairly stable, liquid investment, primarily because the maturity of the notes is relatively short—typically less than nine months, most commonly between one and two months.

Treasury market securities Treasury market securities are investments that include U.S. Treasury bills, notes, and bonds. These represent loans to the U.S. government: they're backed by the "full faith and credit" of the government, so Treasury securities are considered the safest of all investments.

who want to follow the Wealth Plan for Young Investors invest a portion of their money that is not being invested in stocks or index funds in a money market fund or a one-year CD. You can get your money at any time with a money market fund, but with a one-year CD you can take it out only after the one year is up. A portion of the money not being invested in stocks and index funds should be put into either a money market fund or a one-year CD. If you will be needing the money, a money market fund makes more sense, but if you don't need it for one year, you can put it into the one-year CD, where it will earn a higher interest rate. A money market fund usually pays an interest rate above 2%, but it can go lower if interest rates fall.

It's Your MONEY

Focus, Focus, Focus!

It's easy to get caught up in all the investment possibilities and lost in the figures. That's when the work you did in Step 1 really pays off. Knowing your goals and your time horizon can help you focus your search and narrow your options. The financial world is offering thousands of investment vehicles, but only you know where you want to go and when you want to be there.

Regular Savings Account

The regular savings account at a bank or credit union provides security and some interest for your money. When you open up your account, you should try to get the best rate you can, which may mean shopping around for your bank and seeing what they offer. You may be able to do this on the Internet, which simplifies the process. (You can find national and regional averages on Bankrate.com, www.bankrate.com.) Banks and credit unions may charge a monthly maintenance fee for savings accounts. Make sure you find out about any fees associated with putting your money into the savings account. Sometimes the institution waives them if you maintain a minimum balance in your account. Finally, banks and credit unions may offer gifts or other incentives to encourage you to open a savings account. It's an old strategy. (When your parents opened a savings account, the bank may have given them a toaster, for example.)

Don't Get Burned! Don't be tempted by the lure of something free: if a free toaster lures you into opening a savings account that pays a lower interest rate and/or charges higher fees, you may be paying for that toaster—over and over and over ....

I wouldn't recommend a regular savings account for young investors, as there are other investment alternatives that can offer you higher interest rates, such as a money market fund or a CD. The interest rate is almost always lower than money markets and CDs, and that can make a world of difference. It's better to go with a one-year CD or a money market fund, as they both pay higher interest rates than a regular savings account.

The Wealth Plan for Young Investors: Step 3

Step 3 of the Wealth Plan for Young Investors is the final step: keep your money working and put more money to work. This is good advice no matter how you invest your money.

Go for the Interest Put your money into one-year CDs or money markets, rather than regular savings accounts. The difference in interest rates can be significant over time.

If you start saving and investing at a young age and continue that good habit, you'll be amazed at how it grows. For example, if you start with $100 in a savings account at 4% and then add $10 to that account every month, after 20 years you'll have $3,890, which isn't a bad return for the $2,500 you saved and invested.

And the more you save, the greater your return. If you place $100 in a savings account at a 5% interest rate and you add $50 every month for 20 years, you'll end up with $20,892.94!

How is that possible? Two words: *compound interest*. Let's explore that.

Compound Interest

Compound interest is interest on the interest that you've already received! Let's imagine, for example, that you put $100 in an account and just leave it there, earning 5% interest every year. After year one, you'll have $105. After year two, you'll have $110.25, because the 5% interest is earned on the $105 in the second year, rather than just the $100 you invested. In the third year, you're earning 5% on $110.25.

Compound interest is one of the best things that banks have given to us

Compound interest is, as multimillionaire John D. Rockefeller put it, "the eighth wonder of the world." Albert Einstein, the father of modern physics, said, "Compounding is mankind's greatest invention because it allows for the reliable, systematic accumulation of wealth." He was exactly right. It's one of the best, easiest, and most efficient ways to grow your wealth.

Compound interest
Compound interest is the interest paid on not only the principal but also any interest that accrues.

It also relieves you of the burden of always watching to see how your money is doing. You can do whatever you want while your money stays in the bank or with the brokerage firm, earning interest on top of the interest you've already earned! Contrary to popular belief, many rich people don't get rich by speculating in complex financial instruments—they merely spread their thousands around in various accounts to earn compound interest. They also put their money into bonds, which can pay higher-than-average interest rates (as noted before), because they can watch their money grow and not pay much in associated fees. And that strategy will work just as well for you. You may not have thousands to invest—yet—but whatever you invest can work for you through compound interest. And who knows? If you're disciplined in your saving and investing and you make the right decisions, you may end up with a million dollars!

Compound interest is a simple way to earn a return on your investment for doing nothing—except reading your bank statements each month and seeing your money grow. There are, of course, ways to earn returns higher than 3% to

Keep Compounding

Put some of your money into bank accounts and keep it there, to benefit from compound interest, however you decide to invest the rest of your money.

As you will see in the scenarios below, growing and accumulating wealth using compound interest can make you a millionaire! Below are hypothetical examples of how compound interest can really build up.

Age	10	20	30	40	50	60
Starting Amount	$100	$1,000	$5,000	$20,000	$50,000	$100,000
Interest Rate	4%	4%	4%	4%	4%	4%
Monthly Contribution	$10	$250	$1,000	$2,500	$10,000	$20,000
Years in Bank	60	50	40	30	20	10
Ending Amount	$31,035	$484,703	$1,206,660	$1,801,393	$3,778,875	$3,094,079

5% (mainly by investing in the stock market), but such investments also are riskier. And in times when the roller coaster called the stock market has become too much for many people to stomach, keeping your money in the bank is a simple and sometimes fun way to make money.

Even if you invest in the stock market, I would always recommend you put part of your money on the side into one of the types of bank accounts or into the money market fund I've discussed, paying an interest rate of 3% or more, if such a rate is available.

As the table in the sidebar shows, no matter when you start or how much you invest or for how long, compounding can generate some amazing figures!

Scenarios in Accumulating Wealth: Scenario 1

The first scenario in accumulating wealth is one that greatly demonstrates the magic of compound interest. When you were one year old, if your parents had put $100 in a savings account paying interest at 5% and added $100 every month, by age six, they would have had $6,928.94. Then, if your parents had put the $6928.94 into a money market fund yielding 5% and added $250 every month, until you were 15, they would have had $44,867.38!

That's phenomenal, considering the relatively small amounts of money invested! That's just one scenario showing how wealth can accumulate. As you will see in the following four scenarios, there are hundreds of ways to accumulate your wealth.

Scenarios in Accumulating Wealth: Scenario 2

At age 13 you place $1,000 in a money market yielding 6% paying out every year. For four years, until age 17, you do odd jobs and deposit $130 a month into your money market, which is still yielding 6%. Then you get a job that pays $15 an hour for 40 hours a week. Every week, you put $450 of your $600 paycheck into the bank. At age 25 you look at your bank statement and are amazed to see an account balance of $124,029.32. This is another great scenario showing how compound interest can grow your wealth.

Scenarios in Accumulating Wealth: Scenario 3

This scenario is simple. Say your grandparents are rich. Under tax laws, they can give you up to $11,000 every year as a gift, tax-free. You're only 15 years old, so you still have a while before you can seriously concentrate on finding a steady job. If they give you $11,000 for five years, you'll have $55,000. You invest those gifts in a money market yielding 4%. By the time you turn 20, the $55,000 has compounded into about $74,204.58—not bad for five years of just watching your money grow.

Scenarios in Accumulating Wealth: Scenario 4

Compound interest is again at the heart of another scenario to accumulate wealth. In scenario 4, assume that you have one money market fund. You start at age 13 with $10,000 (gifts from relatives) in each account. From gifts, allowance, and money from odd jobs, etc., you're able to add $100 every month to your money market fund. The money market holds steady at 3.5%.

All else being equal, if you just keep the money in the money market fund for five years while adding $50 to it monthly, you will end up with $15,182.73 in the money market fund. This is quite amazing, considering how little work you needed to do to achieve this return.

Scenarios in Accumulating Wealth: Scenario 5

Although there are thousands of scenarios on how to build wealth through compound interest, I'm going to give you only five, so you won't get bored reading. But I'll tell you, reading about compound interest may get boring, but using it to make money is anything but boring! As I've emphasized, it can be one of the fastest, easiest and most economical ways of building wealth.

In fact, I build wealth the same way. Some of my investments are in a CD/ money market fund, where I earn interest on the interest I've already gotten (compound interest). At least you can be sure that I listen to my own advice.

Remember: this is just compound interest. If the returns do not satisfy you, there are other places you can put your money in an attempt to earn a greater return. But, if you're nervous about the market or just not ready to invest in anything in fear of losing your investment, compound interest is almost always a sure bet, especially if time is on your side.

The fifth and final scenario deals with a 10-year time horizon for younger people. Let's assume that you were to start from scratch at age 15, investing $100 in a money market yielding 4%. If you added $100 every month, at age 25 you would have $16,702.30! Remember: you started with only $100 and added only $100 per month to your account. Your gradual investment of $12,100 has earned $4,602.30 over 10 years.

Take a minute to think about that. The best part is that this scenario is not hypothetical; in fact, it's happened to many people. Perhaps this is why Rockefeller was so intrigued with compound interest. And I'm sure if you make a lot of money watching interest compound you'll be praising this idea as much as Rockefeller and Einstein! However, I can't guarantee that you'll do as well as in the scenarios that I've mentioned so far, since interest rates are constantly changing, though you usually can get a pretty good interest rate if you shop around. Find out what interest rate each account pays and what else it offers. Check to see what banks and money market funds pay the highest interest rates and, if you find one where you would like to put your money, make sure they are not charging you fees for keeping your money in the account. In other words, read the fine print. Make sure you get the best interest rate possible at the best bank or brokerage that offers the best services.

Inflation, Deflation, and the Cost of Living

Just when you thought living your life was free, it's not. There's a price you pay and it comes in the form of *inflation* or *deflation*.

Inflation Inflation is the rate at which prices for goods and services are rising. There are many ways to measure inflation. In the U.S., we generally use the Consumer Price Index (CPI), which measures price changes from the perspective of buyers, and the Producer Price Indexes (PPI), which measure price changes from the perspective of sellers.

Inflation

In short, inflation erodes purchasing power. In most cases, the effective return on accounts with compound interest will be lower over the long-term due to inflation's effect on the dollar.

Basically, inflation means that the purchasing power of the dollar is going down, because the costs of what we purchase (goods, food, etc.) are going up. For example, a few years ago, it might have cost $7 to see a movie. Today, it could cost $8 to see a movie in those same theaters. That's inflation—and it eats away at your money.

The Cost of Inflation

Inflation eats away at the value of investments, no matter what return they're getting. That's why any investment involves a risk. If you invest in a money market at 6%, for example, and inflation is rising at 3%, you're earning only 3%, in effect. Of course, if you just put your money under your mattress, it's losing value at the rate of 3%.

Too much inflation can hurt the economy and can sometimes spark the Federal Reserve Board, the authority of the U.S. government on interest rates, to raise interest rates, in order to slow down the rate of inflation.

Deflation

Deflation is the exact opposite of inflation—your purchasing power goes up, because the cost of goods goes down. Some experts speculate that deflation is a good thing; oth-

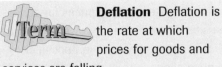

Deflation Deflation is the rate at which prices for goods and services are falling.

ers say it's a bad thing. There's much debate on the subject, but nobody really knows for sure. I myself have not yet formulated an opinion on the subject.

As mentioned above, inflation can be a real drag on investments in the long term, since it reduces purchasing power. However, deflation can also hurt in the long term, since it can occur during tough economic times, when there isn't a lot of demand for goods and services (particularly expensive items, like cars). When the economy is not growing, companies don't do very well and the stock market suffers. If you've got your money in long-term investments at a guaranteed rate, you should be better off.

Ups and Downs: The Bottom Line

To sum it all up, inflation is bad for you, as a consumer and as an investor, and for the economy. Deflation can be debated as being good or bad. It's just like taxes—they can be perceived as good or bad, but most of us hate paying them—whether they're for a good cause or not.

But both deflation and taxes are facts of life for all of us. When you invest wisely, you can protect yourself from them to some extent.

Plans Are Good!

We all know that a sound plan can help us to get things done. Still, most of us have procrastinated at one time or another. Not having a plan to guide you in good times and bad can be hazardous to your wealth. A plan should be set up before you invest, so you can use it as an aid in case you've come to a rocky part in your life or encounter financial market volatility that gets you down on the market. Below, I've indicated a good way to set up a plan so you can stick to it—in prosperous times or turbulent times.

A plan is a very important step in achieving investment success, as you should stick to it no matter what. A plan will help you see clearly in all types of markets, good or bad, and will in most cases prevent you from losing your shirt. The key is to utilize discipline and stick to your plan, even when your instinct tells you not to. The daily ups and downs of the stock market should not scare you into throwing away your investment plan and investing in whatever's hot.

You need to write a plan, stick to it, and execute what you wrote down. Don't procrastinate on writing your plan or putting it into action or you may never achieve investment success.

Set Investing Time Horizons

Most of the return on your investments will depend on how long you hold them, so you need to set time horizons for your investments. Specify years when you will withdraw your money or stop investing and cash out entirely. Those years should be the years of major events in your life, as I pointed out in Step 1 of the Wealth Plan for Young Investors.

It's crucial to know why you want to make money and when you want to use it. You always want to make money, but there needs to be a balance in saving, spending, giving away, and enjoying what you've worked so hard to earn.

Working all of your life and not enjoying what you've worked for is simply stupid—and I'm not afraid to say so. I'm not telling you to be lavish or extravagant, but just to splurge once in a while (the key phrase is "once in a while") and just be good to yourself. You've earned it, so you can spend it. Remember: you only live once. Why not enjoy your wealth and buy what you want?

There are many reasons for investing—besides the main objective of making money. You'll most likely want to use the money you make to achieve a goal or to pursue a dream. For example, you might be investing for a new car or a house. These are big purchases, perhaps the biggest you'll ever make.

It's Your MONEY

The True Value of Money

Money is not just a way of keeping score. You want to make money, but you also want to enjoy your money. Working all of your life and not enjoying what you've worked for is simply stupid.

You can make wise investment decisions only if you take into account your goals and your dreams. You should take time to write down your goals and dreams. Is there a hobby you'd like to pursue in life, a career path you would like to take? If you have goals, you have a good reason to invest.

Invest According to Your Goals

Based on your plan, your time horizons, and your goals, you need to figure out how you'll be investing. You'll have to decide on your *asset allocation*. In simple terms, that's how you spread your money out among various *asset classes*—stocks, bonds, and cash. You should make your allocation decision to fit your individual goals and needs and how you feel about risk (your *risk tolerance*).

Then, within that asset allocation, you select what to invest in, based on your plan, time horizons, and goals.

Asset allocation

Asset allocation is the division of investment money into asset classes—such as stocks, bonds, and cash—and periodic adjustments of the portfolio to maintain your percentages.

For example, if you plan to buy a car in two years, you shouldn't tie up the money in a five-year CD. Or if you plan to buy a house in 10 years, you should find some investments that make the most of the time and not settle for the low interest rate of a regular savings account. If you're a long-term, buy-and-hold investor, you should avoid trading highly speculative stocks, because you will most likely lose your shirt—and then all of your money.

You need to realize that it takes time to figure out your exact asset allocation or how you will be investing within those classes. If you look hard enough, opportunities are everywhere and present themselves in many different forms.

Diversify!

Diversifying in your investments will likely help you generate the returns you need to achieve your goals and enjoy your dreams. Harry Markowitz, who won the Nobel Prize for his ideas on modern portfolio theory (MPT), says that investors who spread their money over various asset classes are likely to reduce their risk and increase their returns. Diversification is essential for investment success.

So, part of your plan must be to diversify. You know the old saying, "Don't put all of your eggs in one basket." That's

Modern Portfolio Theory (MPT)

This is the opposite of conventional investment strategy, which focuses on choosing the best investments. Modern portfolio theory considers the long-term return rates and short-term volatility (risk) of investments. It shows, for example, that a portfolio invested 100% in bonds is actually riskier than a portfolio that's 74% bonds and 26% stocks—and the mixed portfolio provides higher returns.

not just an old saying when it comes to investing: the experts have run a lot of numbers and Markowitz was right on the money.

Obviously, if you put all of your money into one investment and it goes belly up or just takes a big hit, you can lose your money. But Markowitz made a point that's less obvious—and with the figures to prove it. You can chase after higher returns, but after a while the potential increase in return doesn't justify the possible increase in risk. You can also try to avoid risks, but past a certain point, you're losing out on potential returns and not gaining much in security.

Naturally, then, you should spread your money over different asset classes to limit your downside while hopefully increasing your upside potential. That's diversification—the fine art of balancing your investments.

Remember That Cash Is King

Cash is very important. You know that, of course, but do you know why? It's because cash is very liquid. That means that you can use it to buy things anywhere at any time. Try to buy groceries with a stock certificate or put gas in your car with a CD. You could be a millionaire, but unless you've got cash, you might not be able to get groceries or gas.

Those are simplistic examples, but that's the principle for your investment portfolio. You should always devote a por-

tion of your portfolio to cash, such as regular savings accounts, so you can quickly use your money when you need it.

But you're probably wondering, if this book is advocating investing, then why is cash king? Unlike an investment such as a stock or mutual fund, cash is your best *hedge* that will withstand market gyrations, such as the NASDAQ meltdown that started in 2000 and devastated many investors. You should place cash high on your priority list, as you can use it to buy things when needed or to earn interest when not needed.

Depending on your situation, "cash" might also include *cash equivalents*—investments that you can convert to cash fairly

Cash equivalents
Cash equivalents are highly liquid investments that you can easily and quickly convert into cash, such as money market funds and Treasury bills.

ly easily and quickly. Of course, "easily" and "quickly" are subjective terms. But a good example would be money market funds.

Establish a Monthly Savings Plan

The last part of the investment plan is a monthly savings plan. This will help you to consistently put money away so it can work for you. You should always keep at least some money in an interest-paying bank account (whether it's a CD, a money market fund, or a regular savings account), so it can compound and earn income while you attempt to earn higher returns in other types of investments, such as stocks or mutual funds.

A monthly savings plan is crucial, because far too many people find it far too easy to spend all of the money that comes into their hands. Think back to the scenarios in accumulating wealth earlier in this chapter. Compound interest is powerful, but financial success also requires discipline, the ability to consistently set aside $100 a week or a month or whatever you can afford.

Dollar Cost Averaging: An Innovative Way to Build Wealth

Another way to build wealth is by *dollar cost averaging*. Dollar cost averaging is an investing strategy that consists of putting a fixed amount at fixed time intervals into the same security. It's very simple—and very smart. This way, you end up paying an average price that's lower than the average price of the security during that period, because you buy more when it costs less and buy less when it costs more.

Check out the math with this example. Imagine that you invest $100 in Index Fund A every month. The table below shows your purchases over a six-month period.

You've now bought $600 worth of Index Fund A. For those six months, the average price of the fund was $11.25. Your $600 bought 63 shares, so you paid an average price of about $9.54.

January: $100 at price of $10.00 =	10 shares
February: $100 at price of $12.50 =	8 shares
March: $100 at price of $5.00 =	20 shares
April: $100 at price of $10.00 =	10 shares
May: $100 at price of $20.00 =	5 shares
June: $100 at price of $10.00 =	10 shares

If you keep putting $100 a month into Index Fund A, your average price gets better and better while you gradually increase your wealth. Whether Index Fund A rises or declines in other months, you'll be able to capitalize because you're expecting the index the fund follows to be in a long-term uptrend.

Many people feel that dollar cost averaging is too complex. That may be true if you don't like math. But that doesn't matter: just pick a figure that works for your budget and invest the same figure regularly, whether every week or every month.

Many people feel that the reward in the end does not do justice for the work and the time. That's not true. The truth is that the reward is greater when you recognize your risks. Dollar cost averaging works best for mutual funds, specifically index funds and exchange-traded funds (ETFs), which are great for diversifying your portfolio because they attempt to match the index's return rather than attempting to beat it.

There are many investments that should be avoided when dollar cost averaging. It would be bad with a penny stock, for example, because they're very risky and they're so illiquid. It would be bad if

Exchange-traded fund (ETF) An exchange-traded fund is any of a broad class of mutual funds (excluding closed-end funds) that trade throughout the day over an exchange like stocks. Most ETFs are index funds.

it's because someone gives you a "hot tip" and you might be lured into dollar cost averaging into it over the long term, when in fact it was never a worthwhile investment for dollar cost averaging. Remember: the investment return is greater once you recognize and then realize your risks.

I'm not saying that dollar cost averaging protects you when prices of your investments decline. If a fund or a stock tanks, you take a bath. But this strategy ensures that you buy more shares when prices are low, so you enjoy a greater increase in value when prices rise, as they generally do with time. It pays to be patient and not to panic.

Time Is on Your Side With dollar cost averaging, you take advantage of time and the ups and downs. That's why it doesn't work as well on short-term investments or investments that don't vary much in price.

Dollar Cost Averaging: Summary

Dollar cost averaging can pay off with all types of stocks and mutual funds and for all investors, young or old, from all walks of life. Dollar cost averaging reduces your risk because you're taking advantage of volatility. In a way, it's another form of diversification. But you're spreading your money not among investments but over time. When the price is lower, you're buying more shares of the security than when the price is higher.

You never want to buy into an investment knowing you have a very slim chance of making back your principal or when there's too much risk and too little reward. The risks and the rewards should balance in a way that works for you and vice versa. I can't stress enough how many times investors can go into an investment that does not fairly compensate them for the risk they seem willing to take. That's why dollar cost averaging helps, because it reduces the overall risk of a stock or a mutual fund.

Wealth Plan Summary

The following are the key points you should know and remember from this chapter:

- Plans are great! Before you invest, you need a plan based on your specific goals, your time horizons, and your risk tolerance.
- There are various types of bank accounts and all pay different interest rates, so you must investigate each one and figure out which is best for you.
- There's a wealth plan for young investors, though it's not set in stone. It involves traditionally "boring investments," including index funds, ETFs, bank accounts, and the use of compound interest and dollar cost averaging.
- Inflation and deflation can slowly erode the returns of your investments. Be careful and use various hedges against them.
- Dollar cost averaging can be an effective and efficient way to reduce the overall risk of an investment while increasing the potential return.
- Dollar cost averaging is one of the best ways to invest in the long term and can lower potential risk and hedge against market volatility.

Chapter 5

Investing in Stocks

Now let's talk about stocks—what they are and how young investors like you and I can make money by investing in them.

In the latter part of the 1990s, stocks were considered "the investor's best friend." In addition to helping portfolios reap gains of some 500%+, stocks became America's obsession. The technology advancements of the 1990s fueled our nation's economic growth and propelled stock prices to exponential heights.

The blastoff of stock prices would ultimately prove disastrous. Investors have seemingly lost confidence and the Dow is well below its high water mark of 11,000+. Only time will tell if it will reach it again.

So does that mean anything to you? Hopefully after this chapter it will.

What Are Stocks?

In a very basic explanation, owning a stock means owning a piece of a company. The percentage of the company that you own depends on the number of shares outstanding. For example, even if you were able to buy 100,000 shares of General Electric (GE), you would own much less than 1% of the company, because there are 9.94 billion shares outstanding. However, if you were to own 100,000 shares in say, Tofutti Brands (TOF), you'd have more than 1% of the stock, because it has 5,890,000 shares outstanding.

A Piece of the Action

Owning a stock means owning a piece of General Motors (GM), Disney (DIS), Coca-Cola (KO), etc. This means that, technically, you own a tiny piece of the company. The money you've invested is helping that company make more money.

You have rights as a shareholder, too. For example, stock ownership allows you to vote on issues within the company and for the executive team (management). As mentioned in Chapter 3, there are two types of stocks: common and preferred. Common stocks give you voting rights and other basic rights. Preferred stocks usually pay a set higher dividend, but do not participate in sharing earnings, so the price of preferred acts like a bond instead of a stock. In addition, in case of a corporate bankruptcy, preferred shareholders are entitled to pieces of the company before common stockholders. There are pros and cons for each type of stock, but what's best for you depends on your situation and your goals.

Types of Investors

The world basically consists of two types of investors: individual investors and institutional investors. Individual investors are like you and me; we may not be very rich and in most cases have limited capital. Institutional investors have a lot of capital and include managers who run pension funds, insurance companies and other large financial institutions.

For many years it was the institutional investors that ruled Wall Street, often getting news before the rest of us. But in recent years, with the Internet, other research tools, and the creation of new security laws, the playing field is more level than ever. (However, institutions are still very powerful and still have certain advantages.)

We can also categorize individual investors into three groups—passive, active, or regular. Many investors in the stock market are *passive* investors. They listen to the news of the day occasionally and adjust their portfolios every once in a while. There are also investors who chose to be *active*. They might day trade, riding the markets ups and downs each day, or listen to every bit of news of the day and adjust their portfolios accordingly.

Day Trading

This practice—buying and selling an investment within the same trading day—has been around for several decades but became a household word with the sudden interest in online trading.

I have only three words of advice on day trading: don't do it. The SEC puts it succinctly: "Most individual investors do not have the wealth, the time, or the temperament to make money and to sustain the devastating losses that day trading can bring."

The active investor can also invest on a regular basis. For example, pure dollar cost average investors would be considered active, because they invest at regular intervals.

Then, there's the *regular* investor who pays attention to the news, does her homework, and makes investment decisions when she feels they make sense.

Active investors sometimes speculate and take too much risk or trade so much they get eaten up by costs, while passive investors sometimes miss key investment opportunities. The "regular investor" is usually the best type of investor. But it depends on the type of person you are and what types of risks you can and cannot handle.

How Do I Buy a Stock?

Now that you know something about stocks, how do you buy them? The easiest way is through a stockbroker or a financial advisor licensed by the National Association of Securities Dealers (NASD).

First, you open an account with a broker at a brokerage firm. Most people prefer major ones, which give them a sense of security. Examples of some large brokerages are Prudential Securities, Salomon Smith Barney, Merrill Lynch, and Charles Schwab.

Once you open your account and fund it with money, you can buy stock. The way you do it is simple—call up your broker and tell him or her to buy the stock you want and the amount of shares you want of it. Typically, you can place two common types of orders for buying or selling stock.

It's Your MONEY — **National Association of Securities Dealers (NASD)**
The National Association of Securities Dealers is a nonprofit organization registered with the Securities and Exchange Commission (SEC). Membership is limited, consisting mostly of broker-dealers and investment banking houses. Under federal law, almost every securities firm doing business with the U.S. public is a member—about 5,300 brokerage firms with over 92,000 branch offices and more than 665,000 registered securities representatives.

NASD promotes principles of just and equitable trade to protect investors, enforces rules of fair practice, and conduct periodic examinations and audits to ensure solvency and financial integrity among its members.

Term

Market order A market order is an order to buy or sell a stock immediately at the best possible price currently available. A market order guarantees execution.

Commission A commission is a fee paid to a broker for executing security trades. Commissions are generally based on the dollar amount of the trade or the number of shares traded. Also known as a *transaction fee*, a *trading fee*, or a *brokerage fee*.

Limit order A limit order is an order to buy or sell a predetermined amount of shares at a specified price or better. An investor can also limit the length of time an order will remain good.

The first is known as a *market order*. When you give your broker a market order, he or she will try to fill it at the best possible price currently available—the lowest price if you're buying and the highest price if you're selling. The market order involves little work from the broker, so the commission (the fee paid to the broker for executing the trade) is usually very low.

The second order is known as a *limit order*. This is what most people prefer to use, as it gives them more control over the trade. With a limit order, you specify the amount of shares and a price. Your broker will execute your order if the stock reaches that price or better—lower if you're selling or higher if you're buying. I recommend the limit order, because it gives you more control over your trade, even though it might cost a little more than a market order. Most people prefer limit orders. They're particularly smart for stocks that trade in low volume or are highly volatile.

Once you place one of these orders, your broker will either stay on the line or call you back to give you a confirmation of your trade. After a few days, you'll receive a written confirmation to keep on file for various purposes, such as for paying taxes.

Many brokerage firms offer you the choice of buying and selling securities online through their Web sites. This is almost always less expensive than buying shares through a human broker, because you have to pay your broker a fee, otherwise known as a *commission*. Brokers need to earn a living and make money for their firms, so they charge investors a commission for placing the trade. When you buy online, through companies like E*TRADE or Ameritrade, you may only have to pay $10 or $15, which is much less than you would pay a human broker.

Commission rates vary and the best way to check up on them is by calling your broker before you place the trade and ask him or her how much it would be for the number of shares you're buying. There may be other types of fees as well, so it's best to check with your broker to find out the fees that you'll be charged for buying or selling a specific security.

How Do I Know Which Stocks to Buy?

A common question novice investors ask is "What stock(s) should I buy?" While this and other chapters will help you choose which stocks are best for you, you have to perform your own research and buy stocks based on your risk tolerance and how that investment fits into your asset allocation. This part of the book will explain how you can find a stock you want to buy. In Chapter 10, I will explain how you can "research your way to success," which will help you find stocks that have the potential to go up.

Every investor wants to make money, but each of us is different. You have to buy stocks based on your time horizon and the specific outlook for the company or investment you're researching.

For example, if you're 70, you wouldn't want to be investing in highly volatile small-cap stocks, because there's a risk that you might lose some or all of your invested capital. In the case of an older investor, it's best to be a little more conservative, because there's less time to recover from investment losses.

On the other hand, if you're 15, you wouldn't want your asset allocation to be 100% invested in a money market fund or a U.S. government bond. Those investments are too conservative because you'll have the time to bounce back from downturns.

So, investing in any type of security should be based on a variety of factors, one of them being how long you are willing to hold the security and how long of a time horizon you have. The picture you're painting while planning your investing should look somewhat like the box below, based on the planning you did in Chapter 4.

If you're 15 and willing to hold any particular security for 20 years, you'll have to find a suitable match. For example,

Age: 15
Time Willing to Hold Security: 20 years
Time Horizon: 45 Years

you can invest in a small or mid-cap index fund or a basket of carefully researched mid- or small-cap stocks. Either way, if you dollar cost average, in the long term you should make a nice amount of money. Your time horizon is 45 years, because many people like to retire around age 60. In some cases, a portion of your portfolio (usually when you have a steady job) will be devoted to your retirement, either set up by your employer or by yourself or both.

As for the specific outlook of a company, a mutual fund, or any other security you're looking at, it all depends on what the big picture is like and how it looks over the long term when you'll be investing. In later chapters, I'll show you how to research various types of investments. Initially you might want to focus on the current market and economic conditions, but more importantly what the company, its industry, and the economy will be doing over the long term. Even if the current market and economic conditions don't look too good, try to see how they will look for your time horizon, whether five years or 10 years or 20 years. If you feel everything will be OK, than that adds to the reasons for investment. If you're a long-term investor, a short-term setback that won't impact the company over the long term should not cause you any worries. Get a good sense of your surroundings. For example, if you're investing in a company such as General Mills (GIS) , how is the food and beverage industry faring? Are investors, analysts, and other institutions expecting demand and business to pick up or drop? Obviously you want the company to post good earnings, but don't run away from an investment just because there was one setback.

In many cases, that setback will be temporary and, if the fundamentals of the company are fine, you'll most likely make money on your investment in the long run. Unless you're *short* a stock, a type of investment technique I'll explain later, you want everything or most things to be positive with the company, the industry, and the economy—even though some companies still thrive in a bad economy.

It's Your MONEY

Know Your Surroundings

Before buying a stock, know your surroundings: understand the industry, the economic conditions, growth potential, etc.

Market Capitalization and Types of Stocks

A very basic way of categorizing stocks is by size—market capitalization. As I explained in Chapter 3, market capitalization is the price of a stock at any given time multiplied by the amount of shares outstanding. The term is usually shortened to *cap*: companies are generally categorized as *large cap*, *mid cap*, *small cap*, and *micro cap*. (You may also run into the terms *giant cap* or *mega cap*, *big cap*, and *nano cap*.)

Large cap stocks tend to get the most attention. *Mid caps* and *small caps* don't get as much attention unless they're outperforming the market at a specific time. The box below shows dollar definitions (which vary) and the risk/reward theoretically involved within each type of stock.

Large Cap: $10 billion and up—low risk, low reward
Mid Cap: $2 billion to $10 billion—intermediate risk, intermediate reward
Small Cap: $500 million to $2 billion—high risk, high reward

As you can see, in general, the larger the company, the less risk and, logically, the less potential reward. Again, you've got to know what returns you want and how much risk you can tolerate.

An example of a large-cap company is Johnson & Johnson (JNJ), the giant pharmaceutical/medical products firm, which has a long, established history and is well respected within its industry and throughout the world. Johnson & Johnson's market cap is about $166 billion as of this writing.

Johnson & Johnson would be considered a blue chip stock. Blue chip stocks, as I explained in Chapter 3, are venerable companies with established histories and are usually well respected. Blue chip stocks are usually large cap.

Mid-cap companies often have well known names and brands, but aren't as large or as established as large caps. One example of a mid-cap company is A.G. Edwards (AGE), the financial firm that specializes in stock brokerage. The name is known, but A.G. Edwards is not as large as other companies within its industry, such as Merrill Lynch.

Then there are small-cap companies. They're riskier than large-cap and mid-cap companies, but they also have much potential if you're willing to hold them long enough for them to evolve—if they do well, of course! An example of a small-cap company is TriqQuint Semiconductor (TQNT), "a supplier of components and modules for communications applications," according to MultexInvestor.com. TriQuint made its name known during the bull market of the 1990s, as one of the premiere technology-related companies during the boom. TriQuint has a market cap of about $530 million as of this writing.

The riskiest of the group are micro-cap companies. Micro-cap companies are usually startups or ones that don't have enough cash to fund their new products. Micro-cap companies can be hard to follow, because so little information might be available on them and the stock might not move as much as small-, mid-, or large-cap stocks. An example of a micro-cap company is Ronson Corp. (RONC), a small maker of butane products, produced from petroleum. Although it's been in existence for more than a century (it was founded in 1886), the company is not as well known as some of its competitors, but most people recognize the name around its headquarters in Somerset, New Jersey. Micro-cap companies are considered extremely risky, but carry the opportunity for large rewards as well.

Initial Public Offerings (IPO)

An initial public offering (IPO) is an investment that can be as risky as a micro-cap company, but in actuality can be a large-cap company. How is that possible?

An IPO occurs at a time when a company becomes public, meaning that now investors can buy shares in the company. IPOs at first can be extremely risky, because when stock starts to trade publicly, traders tend to trade in and out of them, which causes wild price swings.

Initial public offering (IPO) An initial public offering is the first sale of stock to the public by a private company. That's why it's also known as *going public*. IPOs are often by younger, smaller companies seeking capital to expand. IPOs offer the possibility of big gains but investors must be prepared to accept big risks.

Do you remember TheGlobe.com's IPO? It's a prime example of the roller coaster trading that went on so often during the technology and Internet boom of the 1990s. On its first day of trading, in November 1998, the stock started around $9 and quickly jumped as high as $97, before falling back to $63.50 at the close of trading. TheGlobe.com went public during the height of the Internet boom, when almost all technology companies soared—irrationally, as many argued later. An investor should wait until a year or so following an IPO to even consider investing in the stock because it may still have some volatility remaining from going public. Another reason to not invest in the stock for one year is so you can see how the company reports its financials and how it reacts

Dollars & Sense

Give It Time
If you get a chance to invest in an IPO, pass—at least for a year or so. Sure, you may miss out on a chance to make some big bucks—but you'll also avoid some serious risks.

to the market in general. If you find you want to invest in an IPO after a year and the fundamentals appear sound, always ask yourself, "Was it smart for this company to have gone public?" This will help you judge in the final stages of deciding whether or not you want to buy stock in the company.

Foreign Stocks: The Risk Becomes Apparent

Foreign stocks are also risky. They command a high place on the risk/reward ratio tree. The primary reason they're so risky is because a majority of their business may be in a country that's economically or possibly even politically weak (although not all foreign countries have troubled governments)! Then there's also the currency risk: if you're invested in a company in another country and the currency of that country becomes weak, your investment in that company might significantly decrease in value—even if the company does well. Think back to the discussion of investing abroad in Chapter 3, on the differences in risk and reward between *developed* markets and *emerging* markets, which are growing rapidly, economically and politically.

If you feel compelled to invest abroad, stick to traditionally more stable countries, like Great Britain, Canada, or Germany. If you want to venture out and invest in the likes of Turkey, Hong Kong, or Malaysia, it's best to have a well-diversified portfolio and apportion only a small percentage (say, less than 10%) to such investments.

Exotics

If you like exotic countries, visit them—don't invest in them. Your money is safer in companies in countries with economies that are more stable.

Risk and Reward: One of the Most Important Factors When Investing

Just as you should read the fine print in legally binding contracts, you have to recognize and then realize the risks you face when investing in various types of securities. For example, typically a blue-chip stock carries less risk than a small company stock. A small company in some cases might not even have very many products on the market, while a large established company might have thousands. Also, an economic event that can hurt a small company seriously might not have any significant effect on a large company. Therefore, there's less risk when investing in the blue-chip company, but also a smaller potential for reward. The opposite is true with small companies: the risk is greater, but so is the possible return.

Risk and reward are one of the most important parts of investing in the financial markets and evaluating any type of security. For the amount of risk you're willing to take, you should be compensated equally. That's the risk/reward ratio that we discussed in Chapter 3, the relation between the risk in an investment and the potential gain. But in some cases investors don't do their homework or they get lazy and choose investments with tons of risk and little reward.

Usually people have a combination of investments—not just one—so their portfolio has a better balance of risk and return. For example, if you choose a portfolio allocation of 1% bonds and 99% stocks, don't expect that 1% of bonds to compensate you for the risk you're taking by investing 99% of your money in stocks.

The opposite would be an allocation of 99% bonds and 1% stocks—with the stocks all large caps and the bonds all issued by the U.S. government. This allocation, even though it would provide a nice, steady income from the bonds, carries very little risk and therefore offers less reward than if you invested 50% in stocks and 50% in bonds. The only reward would be the interest from the bonds and whatever dividends and appreciation might come from the stocks. Again, don't expect your 1% stocks to provide so much return as to best the income from your 99% bonds—it just won't happen.

Most investors need to have a balanced asset allocation, rather than a lop-sided one. Either way, you don't want to take too much risk and you don't want to take too little risk. You must assess your own tolerance for risk, your timeline, goals, etc. But I personally agree with one company's ad that claims, "The greatest risk is not taking one."

Stocks: The Two Key Types of Analysis

There are hundreds, possibly even thousands of ways to research stocks, ranging from the no-nonsense fundamental analysis to the "trickiness" of technical analysis. Analyzing stocks can be a time-consuming yet extremely rewarding process. No matter how good you are at the research process, always remember that it's always better to own a basket of stocks than just a few.

We'll get into the how-to of analysis in Chapter 10. For now, I just want to mention that there are a few types of analysis of stocks and other investments that all investors need to understand.

First, the most popular one (though seemingly forgotten amid the Internet stock heyday of the 1990s) is *fundamental analysis*. This means studying a company's income statement, balance sheet, cash flows, and key financial ratios to determine the current financial strength and the future growth and profitability prospects of a company in order to estimate whether the stock price is valued too high or too low.

Then there's *technical analysis*, made much more popular by the Internet stock and day trading boom. This approach uses charts, graphs, and other key indicators to study the trading patterns of a stock and predict future movements in the price, so the trader or investor gets a sense of when the time is right to jump in and out of stocks.

Though there's no type of analysis that investors must use, I would recommend beginners start out with fundamental analysis to get a good sense of the company and its business. For those with a technical analysis bias, I would suggest reading a book or two on the subject and doing a search with your favorite Internet search engine for indicators and such that might meet your needs.

Term **Fundamental analysis** Fundamental analysis is a method of analyzing securities that involves examining the financials and operations of a company, especially sales, earnings, assets, debt, growth potential, products, competition, and management. Fundamental analysis takes into consideration only information that's directly related to the company.

Technical analysis Technical analysis is a method of analyzing securities based on the assumption that charts of prices and volumes and other market data can help predict future market trends, usually short-term. Technical analysis does not consider the intrinsic value of the security.

Technical Analysis for Beginners

Here are some books to get you started in technical analysis:

Technical Analysis from A to Z, 2nd Edition, Steven B. Achelis (McGraw-Hill, 2000)

Getting Started in Technical Analysis. Jack D. Schwager (John Wiley & Sons, 1998)

Martin Pring's Introduction to Technical Analysis, Martin J. Pring (McGraw-Hill, 1997)

Earnings: It Matters

When you research investments, one key figure that most companies present to shareholders every quarter is *earnings*. Earnings, as you might guess, are what a company makes after expenses are taken out.

That figure is the basis for several other figures of interest to you as an investor. From that figure, a per-share figure is calculated—*earnings per share* (EPS). The EPS is more important than earnings because it's a better measure of profitability. It's also important because it's the basis for calculating to what extent the price of a stock is in line with its value.

The EPS is used in calculating the *price-to-earnings ratio* (P/E). For example, Company Z's stock price is $50.00 and the EPS in the first quarter of the year is $5.00. There-fore, the P/E is 10 (50 ÷ 5 = 10). The P/E ratio is useful to compare with the company's historical P/E's, the P/E's of other companies in the same industry, or the P/E of the market in general. Analysts also estimate P/E's going into the future, known as *forward* P/E. They estimate what a company's

Term

Earnings per share (EPS) The earnings per share are calculated by dividing net income by common shares outstanding. A company that earns $2 million for the year and has 4 million shares outstanding has an EPS of $.50.

Price/earnings (P/E) ratio The price/earnings ratio relates share price to earnings per share. P/E is perhaps the most widely used factor in assessing whether a stock is overvalued or undervalued. Also known as the *P/E multiple.*

earnings and P/E ratio will likely be going into the next four quarters. It's important to remember that the higher the P/E ratio, the more the market is willing to pay for each dollar of annual earnings.

Companies with negative earnings do not have a P/E ratio at all.

Earnings are the most important financial figure a company presents to shareholders; even though some people might try to tell you that earnings don't matter anymore, they do. Investors will either buy or sell the stock based on expected future earnings or they will do so after the earnings are announced. Stock *analysts* will either make their appropriate *upgrades* or *downgrades* or leave their ratings unchanged based on earnings news. This sparks traders to either buy or sell, therefore moving the price of the stock up or down. The illustration below explains this chain of events.

Scenario 1

- Company A reports bad earnings.
- Analyst downgrades the stock because of the earnings.
- Investors sell at the news of a downgrade.
- Stock of Company A falls.

Scenario 2

- Investors think earnings will be great for Company A.
- Investors buy Company A stock.
- Company A reports great earnings.
- The stock rises and investors make money.

The two scenarios are just examples of many, many possible outcomes. Earnings can be fairly simple, yet some analysts put out their own estimates, which can easily confuse the individual investor. My advice: pay attention to the average estimate of all of the analysts, but don't make investment decisions based on it.

Never take anyone's advice when they tell you that earnings no longer matter. When Internet stocks crashed in the NASDAQ disaster, it proved that earnings matter a great deal. Most companies then had negative earnings. People who invested in Internet stocks in their heyday lost a lot of money and suffered through agony as they watched their stocks collapse. A company can have no earnings for sever-

Nobody's Perfect!

Pay attention to the analysts: after all, they're professionals at analyzing companies. However, they're only human, so they may not always be right. Also, recent investigations and legal proceedings have called into question the independence and integrity of some stock analysts. So don't take any analyst's recommendations as etched in stone.

Earnings Are Key

Never believe anyone who says, "Earnings don't matter." Earnings are one of the keys to investing success. And, because companies sometimes get creative in press releases to make their earnings seem better, look for the real numbers—the ones that the company has to report to the Securities and Exchange Commission.

al years, but it cannot survive if the company never makes money.

Disciplines of Investing: Growth and Value

Before getting any deeper on stock investing, you must realize that there are styles of stock investing—*growth investing* and *value investing*. Growth investing is buying companies that have growth rates that are higher than average, hoping the companies' overall growth will cause the prices of their stocks to rise. Value investors buy companies that are believed to be undervalued when compared with a benchmark, a financial ratio, or the companies' competitors.

Many investors choose to engage in growth investing, while others opt for value investing. Growth and value companies usually carry equal amounts of risk, except in some cases of small-cap value and small-cap growth companies. Small-cap value companies tend to be riskier than small-cap growth companies, because small-cap value companies might be distressed financially and some may be on the verge of bankruptcy. Their growth counterparts may be in the early stages of growth, but still have some capital to work with. At times growth stocks have outperformed value stocks and at times value stocks have outperformed growth stocks. You may want to invest in both value-oriented stocks and growth-oriented stocks. That way, you'll further diversify your portfolio and reduce the risk to your portfolio if stocks in either category perform poorly.

What Makes Stocks Move?

What makes stocks move? The subject is one of great debate. As mentioned in Chapter 2, there's an idea called the *efficient market theory* (EMT) or the *efficient market hypothesis* (EMH). To recap, the efficient market theory simply means that everything anyone knows about a stock has already affected the price. For example, when a company gets a new piece of business, it issues a press release and the price of its stock immediately adjusts to the news.

So, you might wonder, what about if some people know something that's likely to affect a stock but is not known generally? They could certainly buy or sell the stock and make a killing, right?

Right—but they could also be fined or even put behind bars. People who have information about a company that is not yet known to the public—such as executives, their friends and family, and possibly even some brokers—who buy or sell that company's stock based on that information can end up in court for *insider trading*.

People who believe in the efficient market hypothesis or theory believe that it's futile to use fundamental analysis to search for stocks that are undervalued or to use technical analysis to predict trends. But you should know and remember that this theory is controversial and often disputed.

Insider trading

Insider trading is the buying or selling of a security by officers, directors, analysts, brokers, and others who have information about the security that's not available to the public and that allows them to benefit from buying or selling the stock.

There are opportunities in every market and places properly suited for investment. There will always be bull (good) markets after bear (bad) markets and vice versa. The key is recognizing opportunity and using that opportunity to your advantage.

Don't Own Any Investment That Keeps You Awake at Night

Stocks belong in certain portfolios, but not in everybody's. There are two key questions to ask yourself about any investment:

- Will this investment keep me awake at night?
- Will this investment affect me when I'm not thinking about investments or my financial matters?

The first question is fairly simple—if an investment bothers you, stay away from it or get out of it, totally or at least keep your investment at a level that doesn't make you uncomfortable. That's all there is to it. If an investment is making you sick and keeping you up at night, it's probably not worth your time.

The second question is similar and my advice is the same. You really don't want an investment bothering you or consuming your time when you could be at work, school, or conducting another productive activity. If the investment is bothering you, stay away from it or get out of it, totally or at least to an acceptable extent.

Stocks: A Summary

You'll learn more about the financial figures in Chapter 10, where you'll learn how to research various investments. In addition, you'll see in Chapter 11 that asset allocation is key to ensuring your investment success. While all of this may sound complex, it really is quite easy—but it does require discipline.

Stocks can be a great investment for young people with a long time horizon—and very profitable if you're aware of opportunities and cautious. If you decide to invest in stocks and then conduct the research, as indicated later in this book, you'll be well on your way to profiting from carefully researched investments.

The following are the key points of this chapter:

- Stocks are equity ownership in a company.
- You can buy a stock from a stockbroker or a NASD licensed financial advisor.
- There are many ways to research stocks, though there are no certainties when selecting good companies. You can be certain that, with a healthy dose of research, the stocks that you choose are more likely to pay off.
- The two main types of investors are the individual and the institution.
- Stocks are often categorized in terms of market capitalization, usually as large cap, mid cap, small cap, and micro cap.
- IPOs and foreign stocks can be extremely risky; only you can decide whether or not they should be a part of your portfolio.
- Don't own any investment that worries you or keeps you awake at night.

Investing in Bonds

Here's where I'll give you my ideas about how you can invest at least part of your portfolio in bonds.

Now it's time to discuss an important subject that some investors don't talk about much: bonds. Do you ever sit around and wonder how, in times of market mayhem, the rich get richer and everyone else watches their money go down the drain? The answer is simple: many wealthy investors tend to invest large sums of money in bonds, which pay a set amount of interest on the principal, therefore ensuring a fixed rate of income. Bonds are also known as *fixed income investments*, because they do just that: they pay investors a fixed income.

What Are Bonds?

So, what are bonds? Bonds are the debt of companies, meaning the company has an obligation to pay you back the money you lend it by a specific date. When you lend your money to a company or the government, what you get in return is interest.

How does the company or the government use the money you lend them? They use it for financing various activities. For example, if a company wants to open up an office in another state, it might use your loan to finance the opening of the building.

When a company or a government agency issues a bond, it sets a time for paying back the money it's borrowing. That's known as *maturity*. Once the bond reaches maturity (it "comes due"), you should receive your principal back.

Maturity Maturity is the length of time until the bond issuer must repay the principal amount of a bond; it's when the bond comes due. It's also the end of the life of a bond, the date on which the issuer must repay the bond. Many bonds have features such as *puts* and *calls* that may cause the issuer to repay earlier.

However, if you're investing in speculative and very risky, high-yield bonds, you might not get anything back if the company cannot pay you, so it's best to be careful. If a company or government cannot pay its interest to bondholders, that's called being *in default*, and it's like the company will file for *bankruptcy* soon, if it hasn't done it already. By any name, defaulting on the interest payments is bad; that's why you need to know to whom you're loaning money.

I'm a big fan of high-quality bonds and believe that, if you choose to diversify your portfolio, you should seriously con-

Default Default is the failure of a company or government that issues bonds to make timely payments of principal and/or interest. In the event of default, bondholders may make claims against the issuer's assets for return of their principal.

sider bonds. But are bonds good for all investors? It depends on your need for income and safety. Later in the chapter you'll be able to decide for yourself whether or not bonds belong in your portfolio. But before deciding on bonds, you need to understand more about them.

The Types of Bonds and Their Classification

Before deciding about bonds in your asset allocation, it's crucial to understand the various types of bonds. Some are more suitable for individual investors than others: it all boils down to your income needs and risk tolerance. As you'll see, I explain the types of bonds—corporate and government—and their classifications: large, mid, and high-yield and local, state, or federal. The breakdown is explained in the chart below:

Type of Bond	Classification
Corporate:	Large Cap (Least Risky), Mid Cap (Average Risk), High Yield (Very Risky)
Government:	Federal, State, Local

Again, knowing about your risk tolerance is important, because you need to understand the risk in your investments. Hopefully you'll be able to make educated decisions on bonds and how to research them.

Corporate Bonds

The first type of bond, which is also one of the most popular, is a corporate bond. Corporate bonds traditionally tend to be riskier than U.S. government bonds and therefore pay more interest. Companies are more prone to collapse and bankruptcy than governments, but it's also possible for a government to collapse (as you'll see in the next section).

Corporate bonds can be issued by established companies with reputable histories or by less reputable, non-investment grade companies. You'll remember from Chapter 3 that rating agencies—Standard & Poor's, Moody's Investors Service, and Fitch Ratings—rate bonds as being below *investment grade* if the financials of the companies issuing those bonds are terrible.

Better-quality companies pay less interest to bondholders because they're less likely to go bankrupt. But, remember Enron, WorldCom, Adelphia Communications, and other companies that were once very reputable and suddenly went under.

Another type of company that can issue bonds is a less reputable company; these bonds are known as high-yield bonds (a.k.a. junk bonds), as mentioned in Chapter 3. A yield is the amount (in a percentage) that the company pays to bondholders for loaning the company money through buying the bond. Traditionally, smaller companies and ones with tons of debt and other liabilities will pay higher interest rates to investors because of the greater risk that they may go bankrupt or collapse. I recommend

Yield The yield of a bond is a measure of the income it generates. Yield is calculated as the amount of interest paid on a bond divided by the price.

that you avoid these, unless you are buying a high-yield mutual fund, which is explained later in the book.

Bond ratings are important in aiding with your decisions whether to invest in a bond or not. Bond ratings are applied to each individual bond to indicate its credit quality and how sound the issuer's financials are. On the next page is a table showing bond ratings used by the two largest bond-rating agencies, Standard & Poor's (S&P) and Moody's. (I've simplified the ratings: in both systems, an indicator is appended to the rating—S&P uses a plus or a minus and Moody's uses a number—to show how a bond ranks within a category.)

Bonds can be great for any type of investor. As with most investments, go for quality. The best rating, AAA, is given to companies that have the capability to pay interest and repay principal and are considered the highest quality. AAA corporate bonds are uncommon and only a few companies have bonds rated AAA.

The worst ratings are known as below investment grade—rated Ba or lower by Moody's or BB or lower by Standard & Poor's. These ratings mean that the company is very risky and that it may have trouble paying interest out to bondholders. In some cases, the company can go bankrupt. If that happens, bondholders can be left with little (if anything), although more than stockholders. As mentioned in Chapter 3, if a company goes bankrupt or liquidates, bondholders get paid before common stockholders.

Anyone can invest in corporate bonds, but it requires a minimum investment. The minimum varies with the type of bond; it can be $1,000 or $5,000. Your best bet for finding out is asking your broker or advisor or conducting an online search. If you want secure corporate bonds, you should be looking at those issued by large to midsized, financially secure companies. Again, when you read later on about the

Moody's	S&P	Rating Description
Aaa	AAA	Considered the highest quality. Extremely strong capacity to pay interest and repay principal.
Aa	AA	Considered high quality by all standards. Very strong capacity to pay interest and repay principal. Differ from higher-rated issues only by small degree.
A	A	Considered upper-medium-grade obligations. Strong capacity to pay interest and repay principal. Somewhat susceptible to economic conditions and changes.
Baa	BBB	Considered medium-grade obligations. Capacity to pay interest and repay principal considered adequate but may deteriorate over time. More susceptible to economic conditions and changes.
Ba	BB	Considered to have speculative elements. Future of bond not well-ensured. Capacity to meet timely interest and principal payments may be inadequate.
B	B	Current capacity to meet interest payments and principal repayments. Weaker assurance of interest and principal payments over long periods of time.
Caa	CCC	Considered to be in poor standing. Default vulnerability great and currently identifiable. Favorable business and economic conditions needed to meet payment of interest and repayment of principal.
Ca	CC	Highly speculative. Possibly in default. Known shortcomings.
C	C	Lowest rated class of bonds. Extremely poor prospects of ever attaining any real investment standing.
D	D	In default.

Table 6-1. Bond ratings

most appropriate bonds for the most appropriate time horizons, you'll learn where bonds should be in your portfolio and how they fit into your overall asset allocation.

Government Bonds

Government bonds are issued by local, state, or federal governments. These bonds are traditionally a lot less risky than corporate bonds, but if you're investing in government bonds from countries such as the financially unstable Argentina, the risk can be just as great.

Again, the key is the classification of bond. In this section, I'll deal only with U.S. government bonds; the next section explains foreign bonds.

Federal bonds are the least risky, but pay the lowest interest rates. As discussed with other investments, the rule is that the lower the risk, the lower the interest rate and, conversely, the higher the risk, the higher the interest rate. U.S. government bonds carry little risk and are considered one of the best investments for people looking for absolute safety. As stated in Chapter 4, these loans to the U.S. government are backed by the "full faith and credit" of the government.

When we talk about investing in U.S. government bonds, we're not talking about savings bonds. The Treasury also issues three other securities referred to generically as "bonds"—*bills*, *notes*, and *bonds*. The difference is in their maturities and the way they pay interest.

Treasury bills (or T-bills) are short-term securities: they mature in one year or less from their issue date. Investors buy T-bills for a price lower than their par (face) value and then, at maturity, they receive the par value. The interest earned is the difference between the purchase price and the par value at maturity.

Treasury notes (T-notes) and bonds (T-bonds) pay a fixed rate of interest every six months until maturity, when investors receive their par value. The only difference between notes and bonds is maturity. Notes mature in more than a year but less than 10 years from their issue date. Bonds mature in more than 10 years from their issue date. It should be mentioned that the Treasury Department hasn't offered a Treasury bond since its decision in October 2001 to suspend issuance of the 30-year bond.

States also issue government bonds. These types of bonds can be riskier than U.S. government bonds but are less risky than local government bonds. One of the reasons a state government can be risky is that the government can be corrupt.

For example, back in the mid-1930s, Louisiana's government was very corrupt and one of its senators, Huey Long, formerly governor, was assassinated on September 8, 1935. This ultimately led to the short-term demise and erosion of Louisiana's economy and banks became unwilling to lend the state any money, though the state never defaulted on a general obligation bond.

In most cases, though, governors aren't assassinated and state economies don't collapse; therefore, state government bonds carry risk but traditionally are good investments. If you buy a state government bond, chances are the money you're lending the state is going to pay for buildings, colleges, road repairs, highways, and various other projects. However, it's wise to check the ratings. For example, as I'm writing this chapter, Moody's has just lowered the rating for California from A1 to A2, the rating given to Louisiana. In contrast, most states receive the highest ratings from Moody's—AAA or AA.

The interest you receive from state bonds is free from federal tax. You should keep this advantage in mind when comparing yield rates for various bond investments.

The last type of government bond is the local govern-ment bond. These are also known as *municipal bonds* (or *munis*). With each municipal bond you buy, the money is used to finance only one specific project. For example, it may be to repair a sewer that runs throughout the city or town or it could be to build a city or town's government offices or a school. Now for the shocker, and a disruption to the normal risk/reward relationship—municipal bonds aren't that risky. And, as with state bonds, income earned from municipal bonds is exempt from federal tax. Also, if the municipality issuing the bond is located in your state, the income may be exempt from your state income tax, too.

Again, all of these types of bonds carry risk, but gener-ally government bonds make for very good interest-pro-ducing investments. Ultimately, government bonds are a lot less risky than most types of corporate bonds because the institutions are more stable. Your success as an investor in any type of bond will rely on your attentiveness and abil-ity to recognize risk and then capitalize on what you know.

It's Your MONEY   ***Tax Advantages of Munis***

I've been discussing bonds in terms of your risk tolerance. However, your tax situation is also an important factor when considering investing in state or municipal bonds.

For example, take a municipal bond that offers a 5.4% yield. If you're in the 15% federal tax bracket, that yield is equivalent to a yield of 6.35% that's taxable. In other words, you'd need to get a 6.35% yield from a tax-able bond to equal the bottom-line return from the 5.4% yield from the municipal bond. That's known as the *taxable equivalent yield.*

(In case you're curious, the taxable equivalent yield of that 5.4% would be 7.4% if you were in the 27% tax bracket, 7.7% if you were in the 30% bracket, and 8.3% if you were in the 35% bracket.)

Calculate Equivalent Yields

Here's the formula for calculating the taxable equivalent yield for any yield rate for state or municipal bonds:

tax-free yield / (1 – your federal tax bracket) = tax equivalent yield

So, for example, if you plug in 5.4% as the tax-free yield and 15% as your tax bracket, the taxable equivalent yield would be about 6.35%.

Note that this formula doesn't take into consideration state or local taxes.

Foreign Bonds

There is less information available to U.S. investors on foreign bonds. It's best to leave foreign bond investing to the mutual fund managers. If you can invest in a foreign bond fund, you won't have to do as much research, as it will be left to the fund manager.

Invest for Yourself

Since the interest from municipal bonds is free from federal taxes and sometimes from state taxes, they're promoted as a good investment—for some people. However, if you're not concerned about tax issues with your portfolio, munis are a less attractive investment for you than for people in higher tax brackets.

I'm not advising against investing in municipal bonds, but just about doing it for reasons that make financial sense for you. Know your situation and invest accordingly.

If you want to invest in individual foreign bonds, invest only in those of large, established foreign companies that are well-known for their good product quality and integrity, so you can get information more easily. This will potentially save you trouble and unnecessary risk. The lesson: leave such types of risky investing to the pros who are experienced. Similarly, when foreign companies want to list their *stocks* on an American exchange, they sometimes file with the SEC to have an American Depository Receipt (ADR).

Bonds and Asset Allocation

Asset allocation, as presented in Chapters 4 and 5, is fairly simple. Asset allocation is how you diversify your money over various investments (stocks, bonds, and cash).

I believe that bonds need to be part of your asset allocation. Young investors can choose to invest in bonds to balance out their portfolios—a smart idea, because they're usually less risky and can provide diversification if the investor is taking more risks in smaller stocks. Bonds need to be in your portfolio to generate income while ensuring safety and occasionally providing above-average returns, particularly during those times when the stock market is falling, when people turn to bonds for safety rather than stocks.

Dollars & Sense

The Balance of Bonds

It's smart to include bonds in your portfolio. They help balance your other investments, because they're usually less risky, and they can occasionally provide above-average returns, particularly when stocks are down, and people turn to bonds for safety rather than stocks.

Summary

The following are the key points from this chapter that you need to know:

- Bonds can be great investments, in part because they produce income even in tough times.
- Bonds should be an important part of almost everybody's asset allocation.
- Some bonds are riskier than others; you should check their financial ratings as assigned by the rating agencies before investing in them.
- Invest in bonds according to your own goals and needs.

Investing in Mutual Funds

Mutual funds are the most common investment among regular people. This chapter explains why and how you can invest in these funds.

Mutual funds are one of the best ways to invest. Aside from providing a great diversification tool, they also provide a great target for dollar cost averaging—especially index funds.

What is a mutual fund? A mutual fund is an investment in which thousands and, in some cases, millions of investors pool their money to invest in the stock, bond, and cash markets. The mutual fund is then divided into shares, which have a *net asset value* (NAV). A NAV is basically the price per share of the mutual fund—similar to the price of the stock. For example, if a mutual fund has a NAV of $13 and you want to buy 100 shares, you have to pay $1300.

Mutual fund A mutual fund is an investment company that pools the money of many individual investors to invest in the stock, bond, and cash markets.

Net asset value (NAV) The net asset value is the value of a mutual fund's assets, minus liabilities, divided by the number of its outstanding shares. The NAV is calculated daily at the close of the markets. It's also known as *price per share*.

How is the NAV calculated? First, the values of the underlying stocks or bonds are totaled, then liabilities (debt) are subtracted from the fund's assets, and that figure is then divided by the amount of shares the fund has outstanding. The fund NAV is calculated after each business day, usually around 5:00 p.m. EST.

As you'll learn throughout this chapter, mutual funds are great investment tools, but like stocks, it's important that you pick the right ones and that they are part of a balanced portfolio.

Why Do Mutual Funds Make Good Investments?

Mutual funds make good investments for several reasons. Perhaps the most important is that they help diversify your portfolio. This means that you're spreading your money out over many stocks or bonds and not putting all of your eggs in one basket.

Another advantage is that those stocks or bonds are chosen and bought and sold by a person or group of persons, the mutual fund managers, rather than by the investors. So, you don't have to research and follow dozens or hundreds of securities; in a sense, you and the other investors in a fund are hiring professionals to take care of all that.

However, those professionals don't choose and buy and sell securities in the same way. Depending on the strategy of the fund, they may manage *actively* or *passively*.

Active Management vs. Passive Management

It's important to understand the difference between actively and passively managed funds. It's quite simple, but the effects on your bottom line can be significant.

Efficient Market Theory

You remember the efficient market theory or hypothesis from Chapters 2 and 5, which holds that, in an active market in which many investors are well-informed and intelligent, the prices of securities will reflect all available information. There's a lot of debate about that, but if the theory is correct, you can't expect information or analysis to give even mutual fund managers an edge.

Actively managed funds are mutual funds that attempt to beat the market. Usually the funds have extensive and expensive research teams gathering information on companies, the industry, and the market as a whole so that they can select stocks that will generate a return for shareholders.

However, it's very hard, if not impossible, to beat the market on a regular basis. Sure, every 10 years or so, great active managers like Bill Miller of Legg Mason and Peter Lynch of Fidelity Investments will beat the market and earn great returns, but for every Bill Miller and Peter Lynch, there are hundreds of active managers who are struggling to beat the markets. Traditionally fewer than 20% of active managers have beaten the performance of the S&P 500, a common benchmark, as discussed in Chapter 3.

One of the reasons why so few actively managed funds produce great returns is fees. Fees play a big part in the returns investors get from their mutual funds, as we'll discuss later in this chapter. At this point, it's enough for you to know that those research teams don't work for nothing and that all of the buying and selling by those high-priced managers can get expensive and, in most cases, the investor has to pay for it in the fees the actively managed funds will charge.

That's where passively managed funds (a.k.a. *index funds*) offer investors like you a significant advantage. Passively managed funds do not attempt to beat the markets, so they're typically less risky than actively managed funds. Passively managed funds mirror the performance of an index, rather than attempting to pick stocks that will outperform it.

 **Index fund** An index fund is a mutual fund that seeks to match the performance of some market index through passive management—a strategy of purchasing, holding, and adjusting a basket of securities in order to duplicate the performance of the benchmark index.

Index funds are mutual funds that own all the stocks in a specific index, such as those that we discussed in Chapter 3. For example, the Vanguard 500 Fund (VFINX) owns all 500 stocks in the S&P 500. If you prefer to follow an index with a broader base, such as the Wilshire 5000, you might invest in the Vanguard Total Stock Market Fund (VTSMX) or the Fidelity Spartan Total Market Index Fund (FSTMX).

Index funds are typically less risky than actively managed funds and their fees are lower. Those two points can make them a great vehicle for investors. Unfortunately, because brokers tend to make more money on the *load* funds, they often fail to recommend index funds to their clients.

Term **Load** A load is a commission paid when purchasing shares of a mutual fund (*front-end* load) or when redeeming shares of a mutual fund (*back-end* load).

There's another point in favor of passively managed funds: taxes. Mutual funds are required by law to pay out capital gains each year, so you pay taxes on your returns. Generally, the more frequently a fund sells securities, the more taxable capital gains it's likely to distribute. Because index funds hold onto their investments much longer, they delay capital gains payments.

Don't Buy the Distribution

Caution Mutual funds distribute their gains to investors annually, usually toward the end of the year. If you buy into a fund close to its distribution date, you'll owe taxes on transactions that occurred before you bought into the fund. This is known as *buying the distribution.*

If you're considering buying shares of a fund late in the year, check the distribution date and then wait until the dividends have been paid before you buy.

Many people argue that index funds are not good investments because they only match the performance of the index, rather than trying to beat it. This is not good logic, in my opinion. It is exactly for this reason that they are very good investments—one of the best, I would argue. The reason: in many cases, actively managed funds fail to outperform the markets because of their high fees. Therefore, passively managed index funds that

Dollars & Sense

How to Pick Index Funds

There are two keys to choosing an index fund: decide on an index that makes the most sense to you and then, among the funds based on that index, pick the one whose fees are the lowest.

 **Passive Pays Off**
Passively managed index funds are usually the best way to invest in mutual funds.

can match the returns of the index earn higher returns than most actively managed funds most of the time.

In the long run, passively managed funds as a group will most likely outperform actively managed funds for two main reasons:

- Passively managed funds are cheaper to invest in, because investors keep more of the return the fund has delivered.
- Passively managed funds don't attempt to beat the market, but rather to match its performance.

 **Smart and Easy**
An investment strategy that's both smart and easy is to dollar cost average every month into index funds. Make it a habit and you'll be making money without even thinking about it.

Given those two key points, I hope you will realize the tremendous value passively managed funds have to offer. And index funds work especially well if you do dollar cost averaging every month.

Exchange-Traded Funds

Another type of fund that's similar to index funds is the *exchange-traded fund* (ETF). As you may recall from Chapter 4, an ETF is any of a broad class of mutual funds (excluding closed-end funds) that trade throughout the day over an exchange, like stocks. Most ETFs are index funds.

There are many benefits to index funds and ETFs. Throughout this chapter and the rest of the book, you'll learn the benefits of both and the many opportunities that they can pose to investors.

Types of Mutual Funds

We started this chapter by defining a mutual fund as an investment in which investors pool their money to invest in the stock, bond, and cash markets. Because of the investment possibilities, there are various types of mutual funds. I'll outline the main types, giving a brief description of each and what types of investors they're best for.

Stock Funds

Stock funds, or equity funds, buy stocks, of course. But funds vary widely in their approaches to selecting stocks, depending on their investment styles and objectives.

There are several as-pects of investment styles.

First, a stock fund may invest in U.S. stocks (domestic), foreign stocks (international), or a combination of both. If the style is a combination, look for the percentage at which the fund devotes its money to each type of stock.

Term Style The investment style of a fund states how it's intended to achieve its goals. The style can indicate the size of the companies in which it invests and the types of stocks (e.g., international, value, growth, etc.).

Second, just like individual stocks, a fund can also be aggressive or conservative. Aggressive growth funds traditionally pursue more venturous investments. For example, some very aggressive funds invest in NASDAQ stocks, IPOs, and other startups. Traditionally, aggressive growth funds are for achieving maximum capital gains, so they're usually best suited for younger investors with longer time horizons. Many conservative funds tend to invest in larger, blue chip companies.

Third, style can be based on the size of the company, on *market capitalization*. There are *cap funds*—ones that invest in large-, mid-, small-, and micro-cap companies. Large-cap funds traditionally are the least risky out of all of the cap funds. The primary objective is to achieve above-average returns while taking less risk than with an aggressive growth fund. Mid-cap funds are riskier than large-cap funds, but can be less risky than aggressive growth funds. Small-cap funds are traditionally a lot riskier than mid- and large-cap funds. Last, micro-cap funds are traditionally the riskiest of all cap funds. There are also *equity income funds*. Those are funds that invest in companies that pay dividends, typically at rates higher than the average dividend-paying company. The fund may also invest a large portion of its assets in convertible securities—securities that allow the option of exchanging them for another security at a set date or for a set price—and other types of bonds. These types of funds are best for conservative investors with a short time horizon, in part because the dividends from the fund will help complement an already diversified portfolio—especially if you choose to have the dividends reinvested to buy more shares of the fund.

Another type of fund that invests in several types of investments is a *balanced fund*. Balanced funds invest in preferred stock, common stock, and bonds. Like equity income funds, these types of funds are best for conservative

Equity income fund An equity income fund is a mutual fund that invests in companies that pay dividends and may also invest in convertible securities and other types of bonds. Equity income funds are intended for long-term growth with a limited risk to principal.

Convertible security A convertible security is a bond, preferred stock, or a debenture (unsecured debt) that the holder has the option of exchanging for common stock of the issuing corporation.

Balanced fund A balanced fund is a mutual fund that invests in preferred stock, common stock, and bonds.

investors, in part because most balanced funds won't achieve the type of returns aggressive and more active investors are looking for. But balanced funds are a very good way to add stability to a portfolio, since they tend to do better than the more aggressive funds when markets are going down.

For investors who prefer growth and income-paying companies and bonds, look no further than growth and income funds, which invest in stocks that pay larger-than-average dividends to shareholders. These funds may also devote a portion of their assets to companies that have earnings growth, hence the "growth and income" name. Because they appeal to many investors by investing in both growth and income-generating companies, these types of funds can become a core focus in many investors' portfolios.

Growth and income fund A growth and income fund is a fund whose objective is to provide both growth of capital and a stream of income.

Bond Funds

Bond funds are funds that invest in government bonds and bonds issued by companies. As discussed in Chapter 6, bonds from corporations can be very safe, such as bonds from a blue chip corporation like General Electric (GE), and they can also be not so safe, such as high-yield bonds (a.k.a. junk bonds), which can be very risky and require a lot more caution, as discussed in Chapters 3 and 6. Bonds from governments can also be very safe, like bonds from the United States, or risky, like bonds from governments that are struggling to pay off their debts. Investors generally get higher interest on emerging market bonds (as explained in Chapter 3), because of the risk that the country may default, that is, it may not be able to pay its interest to bondholders.

There are various types of bond funds; some are riskier than others. The least risky is a short-term bond fund, which invests in corporate and government bonds with maturities usually ranging from one to five years. Short-term bond funds usually don't move very much in price when interest rates go up, so they appeal a lot more to retirees and investors with short time horizons. There are intermediate-term bond funds, which generally own government and corporate bonds that mature in five to 10 years. Short- and intermediate-term funds provide income with a high degree of safety and are best for investors who seek safety, such as people getting ready to retire or people who are already retired. For people who need more income and have somewhat longer time horizons, long-term bond funds, which mature in 15 to 30 years, may make more sense. The funds are designed to provide investors with a stream of income at steady rates.

A *municipal bond fund* is one that invests in the debt of local and state governments, as explained in Chapter 6. The interest from a municipal fund is free from federal taxes; thus, it can be good investment for people who pay a lot in income taxes. Then there are single-state bond funds, which invest—as you might guess—in bonds issued by one state. That makes the interest free from state income tax for investors living in that state. These funds are tax-efficient and therefore an attractive investment to people concerned about tax issues within their portfolios.

The last and riskiest type of bond fund is a *high-yield bond fund*. A high-yield bond fund (a.k.a. *junk bond fund*) is the riskiest bond fund, because it invests in the debt of companies that are distressed and may have trouble making payments to bondholders. The fund therefore has the chance of a very high return because of the very high risk involved. Normally, I would recommend staying away from high-risk investments such as high-yield funds, but if you can handle the risk, you can always put a little portion of your portfolio into a high-yield fund as an added diversifier. If you buy into such investments, make sure you invest in a high-yield fund, not individual high-yield bonds, because with the fund you have capable professionals doing the research and analysis for you and you have a variety of high-yield bonds in the fund, not just one.

Another type of fund class is an *international fund*. These funds invest in the debt of companies with headquarters outside the U.S. There are fewer international bond funds than international stock funds.

International bond funds can be focused. There are *emerging markets funds*, which invest in bonds issued by companies that have most or all of their operations in emerging markets like Korea and Turkey. There are also *single country funds*, which invest in the bonds of companies that have most or all of their operations in just one specific country.

There are also *global funds* or *world funds*, which invest in a mix of foreign *and* U.S. bonds.

All of these types of funds carry more risk than a domestic fund. A fund with an international or global focus may be more aggressive, because of the risks of currency exchange fluctuation, government regulations, and political and economic instability—risks that are generally greater in emerging markets.

Other Types of Funds

This last section is devoted to three types of funds:

- sector funds
- real estate investment trust (REIT) funds
- closed-end funds.

A *sector fund* is a mutual fund that invests, as you might suspect, in a particular sector, a specific area of the market. For example, the chemical sector comprises many chemical companies. An investor who wants to purchase shares in only chemical companies can purchase a fund such as the Fidelity Select Chemicals Fund (FSCHX). However, such mutual funds are expensive, because of high costs, and can be risky, because they concentrate on only one sector, with no diversification into other sectors.

Sector fund A sector fund is a mutual fund whose objective is to invest in a particular industry or area of the economy. Sector funds tend to do very well or very poorly, depending on the conditions of the sector.

REIT *funds* invest in real estate investment trusts, which are companies that own real estate properties. They are listed on various stock exchanges, because they are stocks that own a portfolio of real estate properties. Those properties can be offices, factory outlets, stores, apartments, etc. These types of funds traditionally provide investors with an

Real estate investment trust (REIT) A real estate investment trust is a security that invests in real estate and sells like a stock on the major exchanges. REITs typically offer high yields and a highly liquid method of investing in real estate. There are three basic types: *equity* REITS invest in and own properties, *mortgage* REITs invest in and own property mortgages, and *hybrid* REITs invest in both properties and mortgages.

Closed-end fund A closed-end fund is an investment company whose shares trade among investors on an exchange, like individual stocks. Most mutual funds are open-end funds: they sell as many shares as demand dictates and buy (redeem) shares from investors who want to sell. In contrast, closed-end mutual funds raise money only once, through an initial public offering (IPO), and offer only a fixed number of shares.

above-average dividend, which comes from the REITs' typically high yield (dividend payment).

Aside from that, REIT funds are often a good way to add more diversification to your portfolio. The reason: these funds are sound because real estate is a hard asset—a safe haven in any type of economic or political calamity (although they typically fall when the economy sinks).

Closed-end funds (CEFs) are investment companies that trade regularly on the stock markets, meaning you can actively buy and sell them, though I would advise against doing that. A common misconception about closed-end funds is that they are mutual funds. Although I've included them in this chapter on mutual funds, closed-end funds are actually investment trusts, not mutual funds. Closed-end funds invest in certain areas of the market, such as sectors, specific countries, gold and other precious metals, natural resources, etc.

There are also *exchange-traded funds* (ETFs), which I introduced in Chapter 4 and will discuss more in depth in Chapter 8. Exchange-traded funds are investment tools that track specific indexes, but can be traded on a stock exchange just like a stock. Exchange-traded funds can follow a specific index—most commonly the S&P 500, the S&P 400, and the S&P 600—and never actively trade stocks within their portfolios. Exchange-traded funds can also follow specific sectors. In that case, the fund will likely own stocks based on a specific sector index. For example, the Dow Jones U.S. Telecommunications Sector Index Fund (IYZ)

ETFs
Exchange-traded funds can be a great investment, because they diversify your portfolio. They're especially appropriate if you dollar cost average when investing.

tracks all stocks in the Dow Jones U.S. Telecommunications Sector Index. This gives the investor the opportunity to own most, if not all, stocks within a specific sector. Exchange-traded funds can be a great investment for anyone, at any age, since, as I mentioned earlier, it's almost always better to own an entire basket of stocks than a single one.

Mutual Fund Fees: Nothing Comes Without a Price

OK, now that you know about the types of funds, let's look at the price tags. Since almost nothing is free in the investment community, it should not surprise you that there are fees involved when you invest in mutual funds. Mutual funds may be a cheap way to buy a lot of stocks or bonds, but they are not free. Here is a list of potential costs.

Management Fee: The management fee is just that—the fee the fund charges you for the management of investment securities within the fund's portfolio. According to InvestorWords.com, a management fee is "A charge paid to a mutual fund's managers for their services; usually also includes fund administration costs and investor relations."

Administration Fee: An administration fee is a fee paid by mutual fund investors for the paperwork and other types of work involved in operating the fund—client statements, legal expenses, accounting, and answering the phones.

12b-1 fee: A 12b-1 fee is perhaps the most pointless fee that a mutual fund charges investors. It's charged so investors pay for the fund's advertising and marketing costs. The fee was authorized in 1980 by the Securities Exchange Commission (SEC) and named after the section in the Investment Company Act of 1940 that allows a mutual fund to pay distribution and marketing expenses out of its assets. The 12b-1 fee was intended to help investors, because marketing would attract more investors, so operational expenses would be distributed among more investors and therefore be lower for each.

Other Fees: You can be charged fees either when you buy the fund, known as a *front-end load*, or when you sell it, known as a *back-end load*. Funds that charge no commission are *no-load funds*. Ultimately, as you will see in later chapters, fees affect your fund's total return. Of course, the less you pay in fees, the better.

> **Caution**
>
> **Read the Prospectus**
> This is a legal document that contains a basic description of the mutual fund. You should at least read about the investment objective and the investment strategies, the performance of the fund, and the risk involved. And you should understand the fees you'll be paying. Then do the math. The big question: Is the performance of the fund likely to be so much better than a comparable index fund that it will at least make up for the fees you'd be paying?

Mutual Funds: Good for All Types of Portfolios

Unless you're a speculator, odds are you want to build a diversified portfolio that will earn a fair return. That's why mutual funds, especially index funds, are great investments. Because they're investment vehicles diversified within themselves, they provide investors with an extra sense of security that does not come with a single stock, by helping investors achieve diversification throughout their whole portfolio.

Speculator A speculator is an investor who's more concerned about high returns than about safety of principal. A speculator is willing to assume great risk in return for potentially great rewards, by investing in high-risk investments that may provide higher gains but for which the possibility of loss of principal is higher.

In addition, since index funds' costs are very low, investors earn an even larger return. Even though people claim that "all index funds do is match the return of the index," their criticism is off the mark.

Think of it like this. What would you do if you had to choose between two investments: a fund that matches the returns of an index at low costs and a fund that often fails to match the index and charges higher fees? It seems like a no-brainer.

Either way, whether the choice is index funds or mutual funds that are managed actively, I feel that mutual funds need to be in every investor's portfolio—and this is definitely true for the young investor.

Summary

The following is a summary of the key points discussed in this chapter:

- There are various types of mutual funds, some riskier than others. It's important for you to decide exactly how they will fit into your asset allocation.
- Index funds and exchange-traded funds will likely provide many key benefits for your portfolio.
- Mutual funds should make up a key part of any person's portfolio, but you need to invest based on your risk tolerance and adjust your overall asset allocation to fit your needs.

The Efficient Way to Wealth:

Why Index Funds Are the Way to Go

This chapter explains the benefits of index fund investing. In my opinion, and in the eyes of experts and other indexing advocates such as Larry Swedroe, William Bernstein, and Richard Ferri (all well-respected authors), indexing is the way to go. Before I go into the subject more, it's best to get a glimpse into the origins of index funds.

In 1974, after much research and thought, a man named John Bogle founded the Vanguard Group, now the second-largest mutual fund company in the world. In 1975, Vanguard officially began operating and the premise of the index fund was born. Bogle, an ingenious man, had an idea for a mutual fund that didn't attempt to beat the market, but instead to match the market.

Many people think index funds are your best investment. In this chapter, I'll help you understand these funds and why they're a good place to put your money.

Given the market conditions in the early 2000s, it's easy to say that Bogle had courage to defy his active manager peers and introduce something truly beneficial to every investor: the index fund.

Index funds are great investments. Naturally, many of us think of only the S&P 500 when thinking about indexes, but there are many indexes, and hundreds of them are tracked through index funds.

There are many reasons why index investing benefits the investor and why they will ultimately create wealth. In fact, if I listed all of the reasons, I would probably have another book!

You may wonder, "Well, if index funds are so popular and so great, why haven't I heard about them?" The sad truth about our capital markets is that many investors are misled by their brokers and financial advisors and, in many cases, do not hear about index funds. That's because, as discussed earlier, index funds are cheap—with low or no fees. This, of course, is a positive reason for investing in index funds, as you get to keep more of your return, whereas with actively managed funds, you have to give up some of your return in the way of the many fees and expenses the funds charge.

Another question might be "You're young, why don't you recommend stocks instead?" I do advocate stocks, but index funds are the way to go with most of your "serious money." Hands down they win, and they create wealth. Of course they won't go up every year or create wealth automatically. But if you choose a diversified basket of low-cost index funds, you'll ultimately prevail over your investing lifetime.

The Benefits of Index Investing

There are several good reasons why index investing is the way to go, but given the short space of one chapter, I'll provide you with only the most important ones.

Low Fees

To start things off, the first reason is probably one of the most important: low fees. Everyone loves to get something for nothing, but it just doesn't happen. However, index fund investing is about as close as it gets. Index funds are the lowest-cost funds on the market. Low fees are great, and that's one of the reasons index funds are great—because they charge investors about 80% less than active funds.

There are no ridiculously high fees for management costs and virtually no fees for administrative costs or even the scrutinized 12b-1 fee. This is beneficial to any investor—especially individual investors with long time horizons. That's why Bogle is a great role model for me and many other people: not only does he care about the individual investor, he goes out of the way to work for us. That's the work of a master and ace at his game and one who truly cares about the "little guy."

High fees are ridiculous when there are so many better options. Nobody should pay them, because they eat away at your returns. I'm not saying that every mutual fund management company that offers actively managed funds charges high fees for no reason and does not care about investors. But it's rather a case of answering the question, "Whose interests is the company taking care of?" In the case of the Vanguard Group with its low fees, the individual investor is obviously the key to the company. Consider the following.

You invest in a fund that has a before-fee return of 1.14% in year one—but the total of all of the expenses, including commissions, is 4%. In this case your actual return is really −2.86%. So, you've actually lost money.

High fees aren't unnecessary. If somebody in the investment industry presents you with something that's a deal and works out well for you, why not take them up on it? Witness the Vanguard 500 Index Fund (VFINX).

The Vanguard 500 Fund owns all of the stocks in the S&P 500 index. The fund does not attempt to outperform the market, but rather to match the returns of it, less a very, very small fee. According to Morningstar.com, the fund has an expense ratio of only 0.18%! If the fund's before-fee return was 1.14% one year, then the total return would be 0.96%— not bad considering the previous example with the return of −2.86%, which is not uncommon among actively managed funds in down or flat markets.

Therefore, with index funds, you save money, including management fees, transaction costs, and front-end fees and loads. You will also save on transaction costs, primarily because you aren't likely to be buying and selling via a broker. Rather, you'll be buying index funds in an account set up separately with a fund company such as Vanguard or possibly through an online account. Front-end fees will be very minimal; in most cases, you won't have to pay any at all.

To sum up: fees eat away your investment return and ultimately your wealth. The lower the fees, the better your chance for investment success.

Risk Limited to Market Risk

The risk involved when investing in index funds is limited to only market risk, so they're an attractive investment for worrywarts or those who are skeptical about active stock-picking managers. An index fund is a diversified investment all by itself. If you build a portfolio of index funds, you're doing yourself a big favor.

The S&P 500 index fund alone is not total diversification. Owning an S&P 500 index fund, an S&P 600 index fund, a foreign index fund, and a bond index fund (depending on your time horizon) will afford you greater diversification, because you're spreading potential risk into various areas, including small-cap stocks, foreign markets, and bond markets, not investing just in primarily large U.S. companies that make up the S&P 500.

Defined Category for Investment

Another great reason to invest in index funds is because they offer a "defined category" for investment. The only way for an S&P 500 index fund to change the stocks in its portfolio is for the Standard & Poor's investment committee to make a change in the S&P 500 index. Typically, the committee changes only about 5% of the stocks per year, because of acquisitions, bankruptcies, or other reasons. This consistency offers investors a measure of safety, since they don't have to worry that their investment managers are buying and selling stocks all of the time.

Many times, actively managed funds drift or

It's Your MONEY

"Simplicity Is the Master Key"

"To earn the highest returns that are *realistically* possible, you should invest with simplicity. ... The great paradox of this remarkable age is that the more complex the world around us becomes, the more simplicity we must seek in order to realize our financial goals. ... Simplicity is the master key to financial success."

—John Bogle, "Investing With Simplicity," January 30, 1999

dabble in different areas. For example, a fund that specializes in small-cap stocks may drift into mid-cap or even large-cap stocks if a particular stock or stocks are moving. Since index funds have a defined category and do not stray, they are ever the more attractive investments.

Lower Taxes

Nobody likes to pay Uncle Sam, but it's a necessary part of making money. If you own index funds in a taxable account, your tax bill will likely be lower than with a portfolio made up of actively managed funds. The primary reason: index funds don't make changes that often, so the turnover of stocks is low. Because they don't trade much, you'll save on capital gains taxes if the index fund you purchase does well. Your taxes will be lower than those you would likely have to pay with actively managed funds.

It's Your MONEY

Turnovers Cost! High turnover of holdings in a mutual fund can cost you in two ways. One, those transactions cost money—and those costs reduce returns by an average of about 0.7% per year. Two, those sales create gains that must be distributed to the investors—as taxable capital gains.

Of course, trading can at times mean greater tax efficiency, if the managers are selling stocks that are losing value to offset the gains being made by other stocks in the portfolio. But that's not always the case.

Don't get me wrong: actively managed funds aren't "bad." But in most key categories, index funds win. Of course, if you want more risk and you want the thrill of a manager trying to beat the market, actively managed funds may appeal to you. However, that doesn't necessarily mean it's the right choice. Indexing works—and you can make it work for you.

Turnover Ratio

The turnover ratio of a fund is a measure of how often a fund manager buys and sells securities within a year. Calculate the turnover ratio of a fund by dividing the total annual purchases or total annual sales—whichever is the less—by the total assets under management. In general, the higher the turnover, the greater the tax liability.

Minimize Costs

Low-cost index fund investing is one of the best ways to build wealth over the long term.

Exchange-Traded Funds (ETFs): An Index Fund Substitute

If you want to purchase an index fund, but it's too much of a hassle to open up a new account with Vanguard, chances are you'll love exchange-traded funds (ETFs). As explained in Chapters 4 and 7, ETFs are essentially index mutual funds that you can actively buy and sell whenever the markets are open.

However, I would recommend against jumping in and out of them, because the brokerage commissions would eventually eat away all of your wealth and the gains you might have made. But, like open-end index funds, if you buy and hold ETFs such as the Vanguard Total Stock Market VIPERs (VTI), you'll have the same sense of security as you would with an open-end index fund. (VIPER is an acronym for Vanguard Index Participation Equity Receipts.) The total expense ratio for the Vanguard Total Stock Market VIPERs is approximately 0.15%, a little less than the total expense ratio for the regular Vanguard Total Stock Market Fund (VTSMX).

By the way, a total market fund holds thousands of stocks, both large and small. ETFs get more interesting. They not only track such indexes as the S&P 500 and the broad market, but they also track biotech and broadband Internet indexes, among many others.

For example, such funds as the iShares Dow Jones U.S. Telecommunications Sector Index Fund (IYZ) own common stocks involved in various segments of the telecommunications industry that are included in the Dow Jones U.S. Telecommunications Index, an index complied by the Dow Jones Company. An investor who wanted to get involved with telecommunications stocks, but not individual ones, could own a broad index of them via an ETF.

There are many other sector-based ETFs, such as the Merrill Lynch Wireless HOLDRs (WMH), iShares MSCI Sweden Index Fund (EWD), the Consumer Staples Select Sector SPDR Fund (XLP), and the State Street Global Advisors streetTRACKS e-50 Index Fund (FEF). So, what are HOLDRS, iShares, SPDRs, and streetTRACKS? They are all ETF products that any investor can own. All you need is a brokerage account. HOLDRS are ETF products from Merrill Lynch, iShares are from Barclays Global, SPDRs are from Merrill Lynch and State Street Global Advisors, streetTRACKS are from State Street Global Advisors and VIPERS are from Vanguard. In addition, DIAMONDS (DIA) is an investment that owns the Dow Jones Industrial Average of 30 stocks and QQQ tracks the NASDAQ 100 index.

So are ETFs right for you? Yes, especially if you want to invest in a specific sector or the entire market and do it while the market is open. It's a great way to diversify your portfolio, especially if you don't have access to open-end index funds. You can buy a low-cost ETF that tracks a sector and you'll have a significant amount of exposure to that sector yet you can be diversified.

The primary benefit of ETFs is that they are index funds, which make them great diversification tools. There are drawbacks, however. If you purchase an ETF from a full-service broker like Merrill Lynch or Salomon Smith Barney, the cost is likely to be a little higher because of the commission. In sum, though, ETFs are a cheap and easy way to diversify your portfolio.

Dollar Cost Averaging in Index Funds: Why It's Beneficial for You

As you saw in previous chapters, dollar cost averaging is a great way to reduce volatility and to invest a set amount at set intervals. Dollar cost averaging works not only with stocks, but with index funds as well. Dollar cost averaging is very beneficial to the investor, and even more so if used when investing in index funds.

For example, if you wanted to dollar cost average in the Vanguard Total Stock Market Fund (VTSMX), you would end up, over time, paying a lower average price and reducing volatility. If you started when the price of the fund was $10.00 and invested $100 the first month, you would own 10 shares. If you did this the next month and the price was $10.45, you would own about 9.5 shares. The following month the price was $9.10 and you were able to purchase 10.9 shares. After the three-month period, you would own 30.4 shares at an average price of $9.85. Overall, this would further reduce the volatility that you might experience when investing in an index fund.

Buying the Market: Why It's Right for Everyone

So far you've seen some of the benefits index funds and ETFs have to offer, but you still might have the lingering question: "Why is buying the market right for me? Why shouldn't I try to beat it and not settle for just market returns?" As discussed before, almost all actively managed funds fail to beat their indexes on a regular basis. That means that whatever the index returns over the long haul, the actively managed fund usually has a lower return.

Therefore, indexing works because, if you buy the market, you will, in almost all cases, earn better returns than with the actively managed funds. Buying the market is right for everyone—not just some people, but everyone. Whether you're young or old, indexing will always work. It's only a matter of what types of funds you should invest in. Naturally, if you have a very short time horizon, you wouldn't want to be investing in a riskier, small, value index fund, but instead may opt for a bond index fund.

Dollars & Sense

Own the Market

It's better to "own the market"—as in an index fund—rather than try to beat the market.

Beware of Overlap

Before we wrap up this chapter, it's important to discuss *overlap*—a situation that might be going on in your portfolio that isn't necessarily good. Overlap is when you own two or more funds focusing on the same investments or investment strategy. You may have overlap in your portfolio and never know it.

Overlap Overlap is the redundancy that occurs when you own two or more funds that include the same investments or have the same investment strategy.

For example, you own a couple of mutual funds, like the Fidelity Spartan Market Index (FSMKX) and the Fidelity Large Cap Stock Fund (FLCSX), and think you're diversified. However, between these two funds there's an overlap. The reason: the Spartan Market Index tracks the 500 stocks of the S&P 500, while the Large Cap Stock Fund buys many large-cap stocks, including S&P 500 stocks. Therefore, you are over-lapping. Overlapping is dangerous because in times of market volatility, when large cap stocks are tanking, your portfolio is not as diversified as you think. Overlapping is one of the many mechanisms that are "hazardous to your wealth."

Beware of Enhanced Funds

Another potential danger when investing in index funds is *enhanced funds*. An enhanced fund is an index fund that's managed in an attempt to earn a higher return. The primary tactic is to tweak the natural weighting of the stocks in the benchmark index. The fund manager may overweight stocks that he

Enhanced fund An enhanced fund is an index fund that that is managed in an attempt to earn a higher return, primarily through overweighting or underweighting selected stocks and adding investments to the index.

or she expects to do better and/or underweight stocks that seem less likely to do well. The manager may also add some investments.

The logic may seem persuasive. If index funds make sense, then making a few decisions to improve performance makes even more sense. The fund manager may overweight a few of the stocks in the portfolio to take advantage of stocks or sectors that are hotter. In principle, the risk profile of the portfolio should remain similar to the index fund that it's tracking while the performance is slightly superior.

However, that's not how the strategy plays out in practice. In reality, enhanced index funds have not performed significantly better than straight index funds. Also, enhanced funds have suffered from higher expenses and higher portfolio turnover, so they lose out a little on two major advantages of index funds.

Here's the bottom line. Are you considering investing in an index fund that has the words "enhanced" or "plus" or "managed" in its name—such as Paine Webber Enhanced NASDAQ 100 Index Fund (PWNAX), Nations Managed Index Fund (NMIMX), or ING Index Plus LargeCap Fund (AELAX)? If so, research it just as you would research a fund that's actively managed. And don't trust the name to indicate that a fund is enhanced. Check the investment objective! If it says something about seeking a higher total return than the benchmark index, read about the strategies and you'll likely find that it's an enhanced fund.

Index Funds: A Wrap-Up

As you witnessed throughout this chapter—and as you'll see throughout your investment career—index funds make great investments. Index funds are low cost and they help all types of investors build wealth. By owning a diversified portfolio of low-cost index funds, you'll likely grow your wealth more than you would have with a portfolio of actively managed funds.

• There are many benefits to index investing, primarily low

costs and the benefit of ultimate diversification. Also, risk is limited when investing in index funds.

- Beware of overlapping when investing in index funds. It's a potential hazard to your portfolio.
- Another potential danger when investing in index funds is enhanced funds, ones that add or subtract certain stocks from an index just to capitalize on a market gyration.

The Efficient Way to Wealth: A Summary

Because there are thousands of public companies, both big and small, beating the market becomes a tedious job at best. In fact, most investors should not try to beat the market. Attempting to beat the market is not a poison and it will not automatically kill your portfolio, but it can harm it.

For example, think back to the days of the Internet stock boom, which I described in "My Story" in Chapters 1 and 2. The boom pushed many stocks to heights unknown: the insiders got in at rock-bottom prices while the individual investors jumped in at extremely high prices. Ultimately, it was the individual or smaller investors who suffered most as it came crashing down on them.

If you're investing for the long term, index funds are the way to go. The following are the key points from this chapter:

- Buying the market is a lot easier and a lot better for your portfolio than buying individual securities.
- Most index funds are beneficial to every investor, especially when investors use dollar cost averaging over the long haul.
- Beating the market is tough and those who do it once are lucky, those who can do it regularly and for long periods of time are *very* lucky.

Chapter

9

Beating the Market:
Explaining the
Hard to Do

Can you beat the market? My advice is not to bet on it.

Beating the market is not impossible, but it's very hard to do consistently. What is beating the market? Beating the market is earning a return on your portfolio that's higher than an appropriate benchmark, such as the S&P 500. For example, if your portfolio had a return of 11% one year, while the S&P 500 had a return of 9%, you beat the market by 2%.

But it's not that easy. Beating the market is *very* hard to do—and even harder to do consistently. A good deal of it boils down to one ingredient that we all have at one time or another: luck.

Great investment managers who consistently beat the market may get praised for their great stock-picking ability, but chances are they've been lucky too.

The so-called experts on television have a hard time beating the market, and many of them have been studying and analyzing the markets for many years. So, what reason do individual investors like you and me have to believe we can compete and attempt to beat the market?

As you'll see in this chapter, many believe beating the market separates the experts from the amateurs. Well, then, there are an awful lot of amateurs and not enough experts!

Throughout your life, as long as you earn any positive return on your portfolio—whether it beats the market or not—you should be happy with your positive return. If you are not, consider moving into a different investment to try to improve your chances. But always avoid jumping in and out of investments. That's a loser's game that you don't want to play.

> **It's Your MONEY** **Words of Wisdom**
> The market is always right! In other words, what happens is reality. It matters more than theories and speculations and hopes and guesses.

Experts in the Media:
Many Fail to Beat the Market

Experts are everywhere! They're on television, on the Internet, in the newspapers, and in many other media. Self-proclaimed "experts" are attempting to pick stocks. Don't get me wrong: many are respectable experts—but that doesn't mean they're right. The market could care less who you are, whether you have a Ph.D. in finance or you're just an average investor. The market is the boss. You have no choice in the end. You cannot control the market.

The wild gyrations the market does daily can make or break your portfolio, so it's best to keep it diversified, rather than attempting to *"time the market."* Timing the market is when investors make changes in their investments—dropping a stock that seems to be cooling and picking up one that may get hot—often frequently, to attempt to profit from the next gyration. This is not a smart idea. It's very hard to guess the market's direction. It's best to keep your portfolio diversified and leave the timing to the professional traders working for large institutions and the naïve individuals who may not know any better.

It's Your MONEY

Timing vs. Time

There's an old saying in investment circles: "What's important is not *timing* the market but *time* in the market."

With so many experts, it's hard to know who to trust. Here are two good reasons to be wary about any experts.

First, many investment professionals on TV give their "best" picks to viewers so they can potentially profit from some viewers' lack of knowledge. At the very least, they're getting paid to act like they know a lot more than you. It's best not to pay attention to their picks. Many of the media stock pickers happen to be mutual fund managers. If they sell enough investors on buying the stocks they've picked for their fund portfolios, the prices of those stocks rise ... and they look like geniuses. When an expert recommends an investment, pay attention not only to what but also to why. In other words, what is this person getting out of sharing tips that he or she claims can make a lot of money?

Two, when experts recommend a stock, it's rare that the news source follows up to see how the stock has done. In many cases, even these "best" stock picks wind up being bad bets. This just shows experts' inability to beat the markets, therefore, making an even bigger case for passively managed funds (index funds).

Many active fund managers trade aggressively in an attempt to beat the market, but the result is that you pay in two ways, as explained in Chapters 7 and 8. One, you pay more in taxes, because the greater trading activity means more in capital gains. Two, the more the fund trades, the greater the transaction costs and fees, which are passed on to investors.

Between the expenses that you incur and the experts' inability to beat their benchmark, it's best to stick with index funds.

Beating the Market: Playing It Safe

I've tried to explain and support the statement that opened this chapter—*beating the market is not impossible, but it's very hard to do consistently*. However, if you still want to engage in trying to beat the market with stocks, I would suggest you devote as little of your money to this as possible. Failure is a huge possibility, so it's best to play it safe and not devote that much money to trying to beat the market. If you fail and your portfolio takes a big hit, the lesson you learn (or not) will be very costly. If anyone should be attempting to beat the market, it should be the institutional investors who do so for their firms or mutual funds.

Even though actively managed funds may not be the best choice for investment, without them, the investing public would be at a great loss, because some investors do choose to invest in them and also because the institutions keep the markets moving. Even though most of the longer-term money in investments comes from individual investors, institutions are a crucial and very important part of the investment world. Institutions are at an advantage when actively trading because they have the backing of a large firm and, in some cases, they may not pay as much as the individual investor in such costs as commissions and management fees (they may not pay them at all) when investing in stocks and certain mutual funds.

If you have an asset allocation of index funds that are suited to your needs and some cash in stocks trying to beat the market, keep these accounts separate. If you don't, chances are you'll go over-board, eventually draining out all of your index fund money. It's OK to experi-ment, but don't "bet the farm." Try not to be too speculative. Diversify your holdings. Who knows? If you become very successful with the little money that you trade with, you may even be the next Peter Lynch—the legendary mutual fund manager who wrote *Beating the Street*.

Gamble Small

If you do try to beat the market, only use a small percentage of your overall invest-ment dollars.

Why Consistently Beating the Market Is Tough

Many people go into investing in stocks with tunnel vision, believing they can beat the market and make a bundle of money. It's never that easy. If it were, everyone would be rich. The odds are against you. If you succeed, it will likely be only a short-term or one-time success, because—here we go again!—it's very hard, if not impossible, to beat the market regularly. And then the costs you incur eat away at any gains you may have.

When the media finds someone who beat the market, they do not consider that person lucky, but rather a god in the investment world. That's not a good thing, because more and more investors will begin to take that person's advice, which will in most cases lead to the downfall of their portfolios.

If you carefully research your investments, you have a *better* chance to succeed than if you guess at which ones to invest in or follow the advice of the experts. The equation is simple: more in-depth research will likely lead to better returns. However, there are no guarantees. Information travels so fast that in some cases it's hard for the average, individual investor to keep up with the information flow. The worst thing individual investors can do is subscribe to an alert service or a news service. Alert and news services are necessities for professional investors (institutional investors and traders), but they can overwhelm investors like you and me.

Beating the market is a tedious job for the smaller investor, because you need to get information in a quick and efficient manner and then process that information to your advantage. This is difficult, because in some cases smaller investors do not have access to the same information as institutional investors. Remember the Internet stock boom and bust? While insiders often got in early, at rock-bottom prices, individual investors

> **A Web of Lies?**
>
> With the Web, you can pick up tons of investment tips—but beware! If you don't know the people who offer tips in chat rooms and on message boards, don't trust them.

Pump and Dump

In 2000, the Securities and Exchange Commission charged a 15-year-old boy with stock manipulation—making false statements with the intent of moving the market. He was accused of what's popularly known as "pumping and dumping"—buying stocks at a low price, talking them up, and selling them as the prices rise. He posted hundreds of messages to various Internet investment message boards under false names. His messages created interest among investors and the activity pushed up the prices of his stocks, so he made some nice profits by deceiving investors hungry for hot tips.

jumped in later, at extremely high prices—only to watch it all come crashing down, primarily because individuals did not have access to the same crucial information as the institutions or other insiders. (However, if insiders knew of the information and acted on it before it was available to the public, they could be tried in court for insider trading.)

Should You Attempt to Beat the Market?

Trying to beat the market is, at best, only for younger investors, who have a lot more time to make up for their mistakes: they normally do not have much money to lose and they have a lot of time to earn it back. On the other end of the spectrum, it's not wise for older investors to take so many chances, since they should not risk their nest eggs: they have a lot to lose and little time to earn it back.

The choice is yours, of course. I'm not saying trying to beat the market is terrible—it's just very hard to do. It takes money, for the many fees and expenses. It takes time, lots of it, for research. And there are no guarantees that the money, research, and time will pay off. It also takes luck.

Index funds will not always generate positive returns, either. In the midst of bear markets, index funds go down.

However, they are a much better bet than gambling at beating the market. As in the old Aesop's fable with the tortoise and the hare, "slowly but surely wins the race." Instead of aggressively trying to beat the market and outsmart those with access to a lot more information, many investors opt to invest in index funds. Index funds are for long-term investors, because they build wealth the right way: slowly but surely. Remember to take the popular advice given by Vanguard Group founder John Bogle: "Stay the course."

Beating the Market: A Wrap-Up

The following are the key points from this chapter.

- Buying the market is a lot easier and a lot better for your portfolio than buying individual securities.
- Beating the market is tough. Those who do it once are lucky; those who can do it regularly and for long periods of time are *very* lucky.
- Beating the market may have a place in a portfolio, but not a big one. Most individual investors are a lot better off buying the market than buying individual securities, leaving the trading to institutional investors, who are at an advantage over individual investors.

Keeping Costs Low: Something Many Investors Fail to Do

It costs money to invest, but there's no reason to spend more than yo have to. Here's how to keep your investing costs down.

N obody likes to pay for things they don't want or even need. But many investors don't realize what they are paying—and some others don't even want to know. This is the wrong attitude, fostered by the belief that "I'll always have great returns, so why worry about costs?" That is one of the worst mistakes any investor can make. Costs matter. They matter a great deal!

Thinking you can continually beat the market and make up the fees makes no economic sense. Some mutual funds have beaten the market after fees are figured in, although—as you read in fine print on almost any investment document—past performance is not indicative of future results.

History tells us that most mutual funds that beat the market do not do so in the future. There's even a name for this—*reversion to the mean*. Basically, it's a sophisticated way of saying that the high-flying funds eventually fall back to earth while the low-performing ones ultimately improve.

Reversion to the mean Reversion to the mean is the tendency of investments to move over time toward a norm or long-term average. John Bogle of Vanguard has termed this phenomenon "the investment law of gravity."

Expenses will eat away your returns and, in the long run, your total wealth. Nobody likes paying them, yet we do—sometimes in ways unknown.

For example, in most cases actively managed funds charge a 12b-1 fee, to cover the fund's marketing costs. It might be a low percentage, but most people don't even know they're paying it. 12b-1 fees are just one case in which investors surrender their wealth for reasons that are completely obscene. Why give a mutual fund company money to market a fund you already own? As you may remember from Chapter 7, the 12b-1 fee was intended, when authorized in 1980 by the SEC, to help investors. The logic was that marketing would attract more investors, so operational

For Example

Marketing?

A survey by the Investment Company Institute in 1999 revealed the following uses of 12b-1 fees:

- 63% were used to compensate broker-dealers for the sale of fund shares and related expenses
- 32% were used to pay for expenses associated with administrative services provided to existing shareholders by third parties
- 5% were used to pay for advertising and other sales-promotion activities

expenses would be distributed among more investors and therefore be lower for each.

Investors do not avoid such investments because they just don't know they're paying the expenses. By keeping your costs low and making sure the expenses and various fees do not eat away your wealth, you'll be able to increase the returns of your investment.

The Costs of Making Money

The investment industry wants your money. We know that by the ads we see and hear everyday. And they all promise that they have only your best interests at heart.

That's just not the case. If the companies were focused only on your interests, there would be no investment industry at all. Everyone wants your business because they will get fees and commissions. There's no problem with paying someone to help you manage your money. The revenues that are generated help the companies stay in business—and there's certainly nothing wrong with that in a free economy. However ....

It's important to realize that there isn't just one basic fee or expense associated with investments; in fact, there are hundreds of expenses that investors can be charged. Some of these fees are for the most part necessary, but many can be reduced or eliminated by the way you choose to invest. Below are the various types of fees and their appropriate descriptions.

The Commission: One of the Biggest Costs an Investor Faces

Commissions are fees that investors pay when their broker executes a transaction to buy or sell a security, most commonly stocks and mutual funds. Full-service brokers such as Merrill Lynch and Salomon Smith Barney usually charge larger commissions for the services they offer. Online brokerages typically charge lower commissions because they don't provide as many services to investors. Rather, they simply execute the trade.

Overall, you cannot fully avoid commissions. But you can keep them low. It all boils down to the amount of service the firm offers: the more services, the higher the costs and the more you have to pay.

You pay a commission to the broker when you buy a security or sell one. In addition, if you're dealing with a fee-based financial planner, then you also pay an hourly cost or a management fee in addition to brokerage commissions.

Some investment advisors are very expensive, charging upwards of 1.5%. In contrast, there are other investment advisors who charge an extremely low fee, such as 0.25%. That's a minimal fee; if you can find an advisor who charges 0.25% and you are content with his or her services, it's a smart idea to continue to work with that advisor.

By working with an investment advisor with a low fee, you'll be able to keep more of your returns. Shop around and you should be able to find an advisor who charges little to manage or advise you on your finances.

Stock Trades: Differences in Fees for Different Types of Trades

As mentioned before, not all trades through a brokerage are created equal. Certain trades cost more and others less. It all depends on what you're buying and the quantity. If you're buying two shares of a stock, your commission is likely to be a lot more per share than if you bought 2000 shares. This is because there's a minimum commission rate per trade, because trading is based on *lots*.

Shares are usually traded in lots of 100 shares, called *round-lot* purchases. Any trade of less than 100 shares is called an *odd-lot* trade. Round-lot trades are easier to execute and require less work, so the costs of the trade are lower. Sometimes there's an added cost for odd-lot trades, called an *odd-lot differential*. This differential is often 1/8 of a point ($0.125) per share. It's better to stick with round-lot purchases, unless it's absolutely necessary to purchase an odd lot, to make sure you don't pay too much in fees. You can also trade online, because with computerized discount trading, buying and selling stock in odd lots no longer costs more.

How the Investor Can Avoid Fees and Expenses

By now you might be asking, "How can I avoid certain fees, expenses, and other costs? (Actually, you probably started wondering about that back in Chapter 5, when I first mentioned fees for investing.) The answer is simple: shop around. By comparing many brokerages and services, you'll be able to find those companies that charge investors less. Don't be afraid to ask questions. This is very important. Let's take a closer look at other costs associated with trading.

First, how can an investor avoid commissions? The answer to that is to recognize what services you need. If you need a lot of help while investing, you might want to consider a larger firm, though the commissions will be higher. Second, you can always go to a discount broker such as Charles Schwab, which offers investors a variety of services for a lot less than a full-service broker. Even though you may not get as much "hand-holding" or research, many people these days are investing with discount brokers. Last, if you feel you can pretty much go it alone by deciding on investments for yourself, then an online brokerage might be right for you. Commissions can be lower if you shop around, but unless a revolutionary company is founded that offers free trades all the time, you probably won't find a brokerage that will let you make every trade for free.

There are many expenses and fees besides commissions. As discussed earlier, several of these come into play when you buy or sell a mutual fund. In Chapter 7, I discussed types of fees and expenses, but you're probably still thinking, "How can I avoid them?" While you might not get out of paying the fees totally, chances are you can avoid a hefty chunk of them if you do some research, including visiting Morningstar.com and calling or emailing the fund company that manages the mutual fund you're considering.

Dollars & Sense

Morningstar

Morningstar, Inc. is a global investment research firm that provides information and analysis of stocks, mutual funds, exchange-traded funds, and closed-end funds.

As I keep repeating, because it's worth repeating—index funds are very cheap and charge low fees. Aside from open-end index funds, another cheap category of funds is ETFs (see Chapter 4), which charge the same as index funds or even less in some cases.

What Are the Fees Involved When Investing in a Mutual Fund?

First, I'll start with the administrative fee, charged by the fund for paperwork and other costs involved with the nonmanagement side of the business. This fee is virtually unavoidable, but you can avoid it almost totally by investing in an index fund! The administrative fee is very low in index funds—especially those of the Vanguard Group.

The other fee that all funds charge is the management fee, which pays the people picking the stocks and bonds. I don't want to sound like a "broken record" (or a CD player on one-track repeat play), but the way to avoid a hefty management fee when investing in mutual funds is to go with an index fund. Since index funds follow an index rather than constantly looking for new investment ideas, the cost of research and management is very low.

The last fee, the 12b-1 fee, is one of the most useless fees, as pointed out by many researchers and analysts. Index funds again come out as the winner in this category as well, because pure index funds do not charge a 12b-1 fee.

With a mutual fund, sometimes the fund company charges a commission, otherwise known as a sales *load*. As explained in Chapter 7, if it's charged when you buy, it's a front-end load, and if it's charged when you sell, it's a back-end load. Another type of load is the *level load*, which is an annual sales fees that investors can easily pay and not even notice. Sometimes the level load cost is as high as 1% on

Dollars **&**
Sense

Words from
the Wise

Warren Buffet is a multibillionaire and an investment guru whose advice makes millions for those who heed his advice:
Most investors, both institutional and individual, will find that the best way to own common stocks is through an index fund that charges minimal fees. Those following this path are sure to beat the net results (after fees and expenses) delivered by the great majority of investment professionals.

Level load A level load is a sales fee for a mutual fund charged annually, typically 1% of your account balance. Shares that have a level load are called *C shares*.

top of all the other costs—and, unlike the front and back loads, you pay it every year, as long as you own the fund shares.

Yet another type of fee is taxes. Taxes are the government's best friend—but the investor's foe. If you try to escape paying them (tax evasion), the government will have fun fixing a jail cell for you. In a taxable account, you are taxed on your realized gains, as capital gains, and the dividends the company pays you, as ordinary income.

There are many other fees, expenses, and costs that you'll become familiar with as you invest. For more information on fees, provided you already know what fees you're researching, I suggest you visit InvestorWords.com.

For information on fees for mutual funds in general and how much they charge, visit Morningstar.com (one of my per-

It's Your MONEY

As Complicated as A, B, C

Shares of mutual funds are often labeled A, B, and C— which suggests simplicity. But it's not as simple as it seems. So here are some basic guidelines.

Class A shares charge an up-front commission and internal expenses are relatively low. The front load is typically between 3% and 6%. A shares are sometimes called *front-end loaded* shares.

Class B shares charge no up-front commission, but internal expenses are higher, with a declining *contingent deferred sales charge* (CDSC), often for four or five years. This back-end sales charge typically decreases to zero if the investors hold their shares long enough. B shares are sometimes called *back-end loaded* shares.

Class C shares charge little or nothing up front but the ongoing expenses are highest. C shares typically charge a level load of around 1% a year indefinitely. C shares are often called *level load* shares.

sonal favorites) at www.morningstar.com. Also, check out the Securities and Exchange Commission site at www.sec.gov. (As I explained in Chapter 2, the SEC is the government body that regulates the financial markets.) There are numerous other sites that will help you learn what fees there are and how you can learn more about them.

Why Fees Are Necessary

As much as we'd like to deny the fact, fees are necessary—but not all of them! Certain fees are entirely unnecessary, one of them being the 12b-1 fee that certain mutual funds charge.

Though there might be unnecessary fees and ones that can be avoided, there are others that are absolutely necessary: without them, the portfolio managers and administrative people behind the scenes at our brokerages and fund companies would be unemployed—and that means nothing would get done. The administrative fees mutual funds charge are crucial to operations.

The taxes you will be charged on a fund's gains and dividends are necessary to the government's operating budget. Although we all hate to pay taxes and although they reduce the ultimate return of our investment, they're necessary and we must eventually pay them. In a taxable account you pay them every year; in a tax-deferred account you pay them when you take out your money.

Keeping Costs Low: A Summary

Keeping costs low is key in your quest for investment success. From paying lower taxes to buying index funds, there are many ways you can build wealth by lowering the fees that brokerages and other financial services companies charge you. It's important to realize that fees diminish your return in the same way that they make it hard for mutual fund managers to beat the market. Therefore, it's crucial to keep costs low while strategically growing your wealth.

The following are the key points from this chapter:

- There are many types of fees and expenses you will face—and there are ways to go about reducing them.
- Sometimes you cannot entirely avoid certain fees and expenses and will have to pay them.
- Taxes also reduce the overall return of your investment, though you cannot legally escape paying them.

Who Should I Trust? Examining Analysts, Brokers, and Other Financial Advisors

T he investment industry often confuses individual investors and sometimes gets them angry. This confusion is spurred by the fact that analysts, brokers, and financial advisors often care about themselves more than about their clients. Whether or not this is true in your case depends on the type of person you're working with and whether or not he or she is treating you like a lifelong client or longing for a fast buck.

"How do I know who to trust?" you might ask. After you read this chapter, you'll feel more comfortable about trusting some people—and less comfortable about trusting others whose self-interests come before yours.

T here are a lot of experts out there to help you. Here's how to identify those you can trust.

Why the Investment Community Really Recommends Certain Investments

Professionals in the investment industry are always recommending stocks, bonds, mutual funds, precious metals, and various other types of investments and making predictions about what will be hot and what will not. Many times these predictions and recommendations in the media can get annoying and frustrating because those professionals seldom *truly* explain why they are recommending a certain investment.

For example, is that analyst you've seen recommending a certain food company doing so because she truly believes it's an attractive investment—or because her brokerage firm has investment banking relationships with the food company and has been receiving fees from it?

"What harm is it if they receive fees from the food company?" many investors might ask. The answer is simple: there's a big conflict of interest. A naïve investor, or one just not paying attention, might fall for this analyst's line. The recommendation might not really be due to any of the reasons the analyst gave. It might be 100% "party line" to get more business for the brokerage firm.

A conflict of interest is terrible because it shows that an analyst is recommending a stock to the investing public for the wrong reasons. It is prestigious (and profitable) to be known throughout the firm as "the one analyst who earned our firm $50 million in fees." Conflicts of interest between analysts and certain companies are not good for investors, especially those who are actually heeding the advice.

Such was the case with influential analyst Jack Grubman of Salomon Smith Barney, who resigned from the firm in August 2002 after the public and the New York Attorney

General's office scrutinized him for allegedly changing his views on stocks so his company could get banking business from those companies. Grubman got big bonus checks for doing this and his company made sure that his two children got into the right private preschool in Manhattan—and he walked away with a separation package worth $32.2 million. (But there's some justice: he was later ordered to pay $15 million in fines and restitution and was barred from working in the securities industry.)

But it's worth noting that for every bad analyst there are many good ones. There are hundreds of investment professionals who seek out companies with great prospects so they can report back to the investing public (not just other institutions) and recommend stocks with the investors' interests in mind, rather than their own.

> **For Example**
>
> ### The Costs of Conflicts
>
> The Securities and Exchange Commission settled in April 2003 with 10 top investment firms after investigating them for conflicts of interest. The firms agreed to pay $487.5 million in penalties, $387.5 million to compensate clients, $432.5 million to fund independent research that they must provide free to investors, and $80 million for investor education.

Analysts

Who are analysts? They're people who follow stocks and bonds, issue recommendations, and write research reports on the investments they cover. These reports usually go into great detail about the specific prospects for a company and reasons for investing in it.

The best analysts will be highlighted in many magazines and media sources, including Internet sites like Zacks.com (www.Zacks.com), StarMine (www.Starmine.com) and Yahoo! Finance's Analyst Scorecard. (Go to finance.yahoo. com, choose a stock, and then, through "More Info," select Analyst Ratings.) The sources will have a profile of the analyst and their record of success in picking the best stocks.

Analysts can help you to make better investment decisions, but I do not recommend following any one of them without using your head. The best way to use this advice is to first find out if analysts cover the particular stock you might want to buy. If it turns out that the company has analyst coverage, try and obtain the most recent research reports and possibly even some previous ones to see if the analyst has been historically accurate. In some cases, this is hard to do because research may be available only to institutional investors, but it's not impossible. If the analyst has been right, then add his or her perspectives to all of the other research you are gathering. Remember: take analysts' advice only with a grain of salt.

Brokers

Stockbrokers are an interesting bunch. They're like analysts in some ways, but they rarely analyze stocks themselves. Rather, stockbrokers depend on their firms' research department (which is usually full of analysts) to give them ideas. Generally, stockbrokers receive a commission to sell products, so there exists the possibility of conflict of interest in what they're recommending.

There are, of course, the brokers who are genuinely interested in your cause, present you with honest ideas and thoughts on the market, and will try to build a solid portfolio for you. Those types of brokers are the type you want to have on your side, once you find one.

Then there are the brokers who are just worried about

generating a lot of commissions and making vice president after a couple of years. You should stay away from them. An honest broker won't try to sell you something every time he or she calls. An honest broker will try to give you solid advice on the markets without saying, "Well, our research department says …," every time. An honest broker will be constructive with the types of research he or she provides. Depending on their level of service, many brokers simply just execute trades and charge a commission for doing so. Other brokers will execute buy and sell orders while providing you quality research and portfolio management. Others simply have themselves in mind and aim to sell you everything but the kitchen sink—from the newest IPO out on the market (at the worst possible price) to last year's hottest mutual fund. These are the types of brokers who try to peddle anything to unsuspecting investors just to earn a buck.

In most cases, brokers are honest, but don't expect too much from them. I don't mean to say bad things about brokers, because there are so many good ones, but you should know that just about anyone can become a stockbroker simply by passing a relatively easy exam.

It's Your MONEY

The Exam

To become a stockbroker, a candidate must pass the Series 7 Exam, administered by the National Association of Securities Dealers. The exam takes six hours and consists of 250 questions that cover the regulations and the concepts of the securities markets. Those who pass it are then "registered representatives" allowed to sell stocks, bonds, mutual funds, and various other investment products.

In most states, stockbrokers must also pass the Series 63 Exam, more officially known as the Uniform Securities Agent State Law Examination, developed by the North American Securities Administrators Association, in cooperation with representatives of the securities industry and industry associations.

Financial Planners

Financial planners are professionals who help their clients analyze their financial circumstances, identify their financial goals, and establish a program to achieve their financial objectives. They aim to provide clients with model portfolios, asset allocation models, and various other types of strategies to help their clients build wealth over time. They may conduct their own research on various types of investments and they may give you advice on taxes, estates, and other types of financial events that take place in your life.

Financial planners usually provide more services to investors than stockbrokers. But it's important to realize that there are two types of financial planners. One is the *commission-based* financial planner, who acts much like a broker and sells products; the other type is the *fee-only* financial planner, who charges a fee for managing clients' assets or giving advice.

Fee-only is probably the best type of financial planner for a person who needs a lot of guidance when investing and

It's Your Money

How Do You Pay and Why?

Commission-based planners are compensated by commissions on the financial products you buy from them. These planners will generally prepare a financial plan for you at no charge. However, these plans are usually not comprehensive financial plans and they tend to promote products sold by the company with which the planners are affiliated.

Fee-based planners are compensated for the work they do, either on an hourly basis or, in some cases, in terms of a percentage of your assets. These planners will generally prepare a comprehensive plan. However, these planners can be expensive.

Many planners are compensated using a combination of commissions and fees. You can choose to pay for the plan directly or by buying financial products through them.

managing certain assets. The problem with commission-based financial planners is that they too can be more concerned about commissions than about building a financial plan for you and advising you on your finances. That's why I recommend fee-only financial planners: since they charge you (sometimes hourly) for their services, there's no potential conflict of interest.

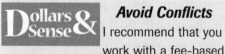

Avoid Conflicts
I recommend that you work with a fee-based planner. He or she will cost more up front, but you can be sure that this person is developing a plan that works for you and not primarily to make commissions. It may well be worth it to pay to avoid any potential conflict of interest.

However, even though the potential conflict of interest is diminished, it's essential to realize that some fee-only financial planners aren't perfect either: many will fight among themselves to get your business. The most important thing to remember about financial planners is how much service they provide you and whether or not they truly have your best interests at heart. You'll want an honest planner who can help you in tough times and prosperous ones as well. Choose your planner wisely.

Research: Conflicts of Interest and Independence

There are two types of research providers. The first are firms that have investment banking operations and sometimes do business with companies they cover, therefore creating a potential conflict of interest. Examples are Merrill Lynch and Salomon Smith Barney. The other type of research provider is independent: they don't have any investment banking relationships and, for the most part, provide investors with unbiased research. So this means that the investor can always profit from the advice, right?

Wrong! It's always hard to profit from any type of research given, but it can be easy to make money from independent research because some conflicts of interest are taken out of the equation. As with all research providers, don't take their "buy, sell, or hold" advice; use what they conclude to aid in your research. Even if there's no investment banking relationship, there may be other potential conflicts of interest, though the research may be more useful and more free of conflict than research by firms with investment banking relationships with the companies they cover. Companies sometimes pay research firms directly to write glowing reports. This is all legal—as long as it's disclosed in the fine print at the end of the report.

When an analyst appears on a TV network, many times the anchor will ask the analyst if he or she or a family member owns the stock that he or she is recommending. This is to alert investors to any conflict of interest, in the interest of full disclosure. Many TV networks started doing this after insider trading scandals have come into the public eye. The SEC, the regulating body of the financial markets, and state attorneys general have been pressing the media to disclose what type of position analysts and their firms might have in the stock. Since analyst research varies from firm to firm, it's best to sample a bit of each piece of research, if you can, and then decide for yourself if there are conflicts of interest and whether or not you want to use the research.

Who Should I Trust? A Summary

When investing, you must distinguish the good people from the bad. Who has your best interests at heart? Wall Street isn't always a friendly place and there aren't always going to be people holding your hand through the process. It's important to recognize that there are people who are going to help you and others who are going to hurt you. Of course, you want the ones who are going to do you good.

Everywhere you look, there are potential conflicts of interest and possible shady dealings. You can help other investors like yourself. If you spot a scam in the investment community and you're sure about it, contact the SEC Complaint Center—www.sec.gov/complaint.shtml—or the Better Business Bureau—www.bbb.org—and tell them what happened.

Overall, you need to do your research on both your investments and potential investments and the people who are going to advise you on your finances. If you choose good advisors, you'll be able to learn a lot more and hopefully profit from what your advisors have to say. The following are the key points from this chapter:

- Investors need to be aware that sometimes analysts are not truthful and are interested only in making money for themselves and the firm. Be careful!
- There are many good financial planners and brokers out there. Using the information in this chapter, you'll be able to select the best ones for your needs.
- There are two basic types of financial planners, fee-based and commission-based. Know what they offer and how it fits your needs.
- There is quality research that analysts produce. See which analysts you like and follow them and their research and conclusions, *but not their buy, sell and hold recommendations.*

Research Your Way to Success and Understanding Asset Allocation

I f you're ready to buy a stock, a bond, or a mutual fund, you can't just guess about which would be the right investment. You have to carefully research each and every aspect of your portfolio and determine if a potential investment will fit in your broader asset allocation plan.

The first section of this chapter is devoted to asset allocation and suggests model portfolios for specific age groups. It is very important to strategically build an asset allocation plan, because a good plan enables you to hold up during bear markets and ultimately prosper.

J ust like in school, doing your homework pays off in investing. Here I'll give you some ideas about what kind of homework you should do.

Know Yourself

The advice that was carved in stone at Delphi in ancient Greek—"Know yourself"—is still very good advice more than two thousand years later. It's relatively easy for most investors to outline their goals and to plot their time horizon. But many find it harder to express their ability to deal with risk. Financial advisors talk in terms of "aggressive" and "moderate" and "conservative," but these words have various meanings. They're just words until you can arrive at a percentage for each asset class in your portfolio.

Second, this chapter will help you figure out how to research stocks. By examining the financials of a company, you can perhaps detect if management might be putting a spin on the company's financial condition. Third, we'll look at researching the various types of bonds—government, corporate, municipal, and high-yield.

Before we get into stocks and bonds (mutual funds were discussed in previous chapters), I'd like to stress again the three main fundamental factors in your asset allocation strategy: you must know your goals, your time horizon, and your risk tolerance. I can explain asset allocation and advise you on researching potential investments, but only you know your goals and your time horizon and only you can determine your risk tolerance.

Keep Your Balance

Caution

Once you've decided on the asset allocation that makes the most sense in terms of your goals, time horizon, and risk tolerance, you should review your portfolio regularly to maintain that balance. You may begin, for example, with 80% in stock funds, 15% in bond funds, and 5% in money market funds. A year later, your stocks have done better than your bonds and you find that your allocation is now 85%, 9%, and 6%. It's probably wise to adjust your portfolio to get back into the balance you determined—but only after considering if that allocation still makes sense.

If you're having trouble assessing your risk tolerance, you can search the Web for "risk tolerance quiz" and "risk tolerance test" and find dozens. Take a few and compare the results.

Stocks—Fitting into Your Asset Allocation

As I pointed out in Chapter 5, the place of stocks in your portfolio depends on the type of person you are, the types of risks you can and cannot handle, and your time horizon. Then, you need to consider the specific outlook for the company or investment you're researching.

If you're going to invest in stocks, then it's important to learn how to research them correctly and how to fit them into your portfolio. Before we go into this in detail, I would advise everyone that investing in individual stocks and bonds is a way of speculating. As I've said before, investing in just one or two stocks can create a large amount of risk and you could lose all of your money, if you don't keep reevaluating your situation.

As discussed in Chapter 5, stocks are individual ownership slices of a company. If you devote some portion of your asset allocation plan to individual stocks, then you may be are able to increase upside potential, while taking on more risk. As you know, the smaller the company, the riskier it is.

As you remember from Chapter 9, "What's important is not *timing* the market but *time* in the market." Rather than trying to time the market, it's wiser to hold stocks. As we discussed earlier, timing is the wrong way to approach investing, in part because the trading costs stack up and eventually limit your upside. Buying and holding stocks is therefore the better approach. You could possibly even

It's Your MONEY

Another Advantage of Averaging

There's one advantage of dollar cost averaging that becomes more important with stocks: the psychological. When stock prices are falling, most investors find it difficult to overcome their anxieties and buy more shares. But if you stick to a strategy of dollar cost averaging, you know that lower prices are an opportunity to buy even more shares, which helps you ignore emotional reactions and continue investing.

dollar cost average to reduce risk and potential volatility.

Since you're going to buy and hold stocks, it's crucial to decide what percentage of stocks should make up your portfolio. You should allocate to individual stocks only if you have a higher tolerance for risk and if you have a longer time horizon. For example, a 30-year-old might want 60%-70% of his or her portfolio in individual stocks. But someone near retirement wouldn't be smart to invest so much in individual stocks. When in or near retirement, it's a lot better to own more bonds, which will provide a steady stream of income when it's most crucial. However, many older people invest in other investments than bonds, because they're planning for their children and grandchildren to inherit their investments and they know their children and grandchildren have a longer investing time horizon.

In his book, *Winning the Loser's Game*, Charlie Ellis says: "Moreover, while an elderly investor may not expect to live for long, the investments—after being inherited by the beneficiaries—may have a very long-term mission. There may be no reason to limit the time horizon of the investments to the owner's lifetime when the owner's true objectives—providing for children, spouse or alma mater—have a much longer-term horizon." It all depends on your own situation and where you feel your money should be going.

Any final choice should be tailored according to your individual goals and overall financial situation; bonds may be the solution so they can provide income in retirement or other investments may make sense if you're planning to leave investments to heirs or other beneficiaries, such as charities or other organizations.

Bonds—Fitting into Your Asset Allocation

Bonds, like stocks, should be a crucial part of your portfolio. Low-risk bonds traditionally provide steady streams of income in almost any condition. As such, they're very good investments for people in all types of situations. But they can be an extremely important part of a portfolio for investors near retirement and those already retired. If you need income and are looking for something to provide you with a healthy interest rate, chances are you'll like certain government bonds and highly rated corporate bonds. This chapter can help you find out more about these investment possibilities.

Bonds as a Buffer

How comfortable are you with ups and downs? Lewis Schiff, a columnist for *CNN/Money*, offered this advice to a young investor (October 1, 2002):

In general, I believe that most investors who have time horizons of at least five to 10 years can afford to be completely in stocks—unless they just can't stomach the volatility that an all-stock portfolio has these days. In that case, a small percentage of bonds will help a good bit in smoothing out those swings.

It's important to invest based on your individual goals and need for income, risk, and your overall financial situation. If you strategically build a solid asset allocation plan with a diversified portfolio of investments, you'll be able to weather all types of markets.

Mutual Funds—Fitting into Your Asset Allocation

Mutual funds are one of the best ways to invest, as I pointed out in Chapter 7. First, they help diversify your portfolio. Second, you can buy into dozens or hundreds of companies without going to the effort of researching each company, because the mutual fund managers are doing that work for you.

So, mutual funds are a good idea—and index funds are even better. Since index funds are cheap and, as studies show, prove to be better investments over the long term than actively managed funds, I urge every investor to devote more of their asset allocation to index funds. Mutual funds (or ETFs and other baskets of stocks) should be an integral part of every investor's portfolio, in part because they will likely outperform your stock picks over the long term.

You know from Chapter 7 that funds can invest in stocks, bonds, and real estate investment trusts, to mention the three primary areas. There are so many mutual funds that you can choose whatever makes the most sense for you and your situation in terms of returns and risks. For example, older investors will likely invest more in bond index funds, to reduce the risk in their portfolio. Younger investors may invest more in stock funds, to achieve higher returns.

Take Advantage of Time

Younger investors, with a much longer time horizon, can own a greater percentage of stocks than investors who are nearer to retirement, especially aggressive growth funds, which offer the chance for achieving maximum gains. However, such funds should make up only a limited part of your portfolio. You should concentrate on building a diversified portfolio of index funds, even if it may not be the popular course of action to be taking.

Actively managed funds should not be a big part of your portfolio, because many fail to beat the market consistently. It's best to limit the amount invested in actively managed funds, though it can be important to have a few to round out a portfolio of passively managed funds. Overall, I would recommend that every investor own a basket of index funds as his or her core holdings. The types of index funds you choose for your allocation should fit your risk tolerance and overall investment agenda.

Sizing Up Asset Allocation

Never guess when building an investment portfolio. To build a successful asset allocation plan, you need to be prepared for down markets but also positioned to prosper when markets are booming. By strategically placing your money in different types of investments according to your goals and preferences, you will ultimately be successful.

Richard A. Ferri, CFA, the president and senior portfolio manager for Portfolio Solutions in Troy, Michigan, and author of the book, *All About Index Funds*, says, "Sit down and assess what the money is going to be used for. Determine how much the pot needs to grow for you to be comfortable in retirement. A lot of people don't crunch the numbers to get the right stock/bond allocation that provides the highest chance of meeting their goals."

Let Time Work for You

Give your investments time to work for you. Don't be quick to make changes in your portfolio. Moving in and out of investments is market timing—and it doesn't work for you.

Investing according to just one factor, such as your age, is absurd. You need to consider everything, including your age, your goals, and your tolerance for risk. You're the only person who can address your own needs and wants and you have to learn how you can go about achieving them. And once you've got your portfolio allocated properly for your situation, give your investments time to work for you. Don't be quick to make changes. You never want to try to move in and out of investments, because that's market timing—and market timing doesn't work.

Researching Investments: How to Analyze Stocks and Bonds

As I've stressed before in this book, you can't just go around buying any type of investment: that's guessing. There are efficient ways to conduct research on investments, so you ultimately have a better chance to profit from what you have learned.

You have to be inquisitive and ask questions of everybody—analysts, advisors, management, and anyone else who is familiar with what you're researching. You need to have a solid understanding of the fundamentals, the fee structure (costs to buy, ongoing costs, costs to sell), the tax implications, the risks, and naturally how it will fit into your asset allocation plan—before you make an investment. You can then act upon all of the information you have received—or *not act* if the time or fundamentals are not right and it appears that the investment won't make a good long-term choice. One of the most important pieces of advice for investors is to try and research every potential investment.

Fundamentals This term is used generically for any of the measures used to relate the price of an investment with the financial strength, performance, and/or growth potential of the company or the country.

The following sections will tell you how to research stocks and bonds and what to look for in good investments. Remember: even with all of the research you do, there's no guarantee you'll succeed. There are many variables and outcomes and, until someone finds the perfect mix of research and analysis, it's highly possible, even with the best of research, to lose money.

Researching Stocks

While researching stocks won't guarantee you'll come out successful in the end, it will give you a positive feeling. You'll learn a lot about the company, the industry, and the economy. Even in the case something happens and the investment takes a hit, you'll still know that you performed solid research and that you did your best. Sometimes bad things happen that no amount of research could predict.

Stocks are perhaps the most complex investment to research. Aside from looking over financial statements that the company files through the SEC and questioning people who are familiar with the company, there are many other steps an investor must take before making any formal investment decision. Research is not easy, but it can be fun to do and it's extremely rewarding when you do it right. The following is a method I've used to research stocks.

Step 1: Set Criteria to Identify Companies

First, you need to decide which companies you want to research. The best way to do this is to set criteria and stick to those criteria. For example, if you want to purchase only a company with a 15% annual earnings growth rate, then you should use a stock screener to help you identify those stocks that meet that criterion.

There are three great Web sites that have good stock screeners: MultexInvestor.com, Moneycentral.MSN.com, and StockScreener.com. These sites are very useful in helping investors set criteria and screen for companies that fit that criteria. After you set your criteria and find a company you like, you're able to move to step two.

Step 2: Investigate the Company

Try to find out everything there is to know about the company. To start, you should visit the SEC at www.sec.gov and the Web site of the company you're going to research. Take a look at their financials, available on the SEC's Web site,

10-K Form 10-K is a report similar to the annual report, except that it contains more detailed information about the company's business, finances, management, and information about any lawsuits involving the company. All publicly traded companies are required to file a 10-K report each year with the SEC.

10-Q Form 10-Q is an unaudited report of financial results for the quarter, noting any significant changes or "material events." It's much less comprehensive than the 10-K that companies must file annually. All publicly traded companies are required to file a 10-Q report each quarter with the SEC.

Books on Analyzing Financial Statements

Here are three books that can help you get into analyzing financial statements:

Analysis of Financial Statements, Pamela P. Peterson and Frank J. Fabozzi, (New York: John Wiley & Sons, 1999)

Keys to Reading an Annual Report, 3rd edition, Ralph E. Welton and George Thomas Friedlob (Chicago: Barron's Educational Series, 2001)

The Interpretation of Financial Statements, Benjamin Graham and Spencer B. Meredith (New York: HarperBusiness, 1998)

through EDGAR (the Electronic Data Gathering, Analysis, and Retrieval system). There you will find all of the company's financial filings, including its 10-K (annual report) and 10-Q (quarterly report).

If that's too much information and you want only the financial numbers, you can get them from finance.yahoo.com. Type in a stock symbol and choose "Basic"; then, in the little summary table that comes up, click on the "Financials" link. Or, in the same table, click on the "SEC Filings" link for reports filed with the SEC.

A lot of this data may not make sense to you, so I suggest going to a library and finding an easy-to-read book about financial statement analysis. There are several good books on the subject. Second, read all recent press releases and other information that may be available from the company and other sources; it can tell you a lot about lawsuits, new products, and new relationships with other companies.

Examining What Management Says

If you spot anything in the SEC filings in which the management says something like "We may not have enough cash to fund operations," you should seriously consider avoiding investing in that company. It is probably in a dire condition and might file for bankruptcy soon; it's stating in its filings that it may not have enough money to continue operating.

What management says is very crucial. If executives are positive on the outlook for the growth and earnings and buying shares for themselves, you can take that as a positive factor and a reason for possible investment in the company. (Visit finance.yahoo.com, choose a company, and click on the "Insider" link in the table.) Then again, if management is too bullish or too negative, something might be wrong. As the case of Enron shows, when management is too bullish, the company's collapse could be just around the corner. Other information, thoughts, and views from management can be available on the company's Web site or in press releases and in its annual reports.

Examining the Company's Financials

If you're looking at a company's financials, you'll want to make sure a few key factors are present. First, make sure their revenue has grown consecutively. If there are any big swings, such as revenue of $10 million in the second quarter and $200 million in the third quarter, you'll want to e-mail the company ("investor relations") or possibly even an analyst who covers the company to help explain the situation to you.

Next, examine the company's *price-to-earnings* (P/E) *ratio*, which is calculated (as explained in Chapter 5) by dividing the companies earnings from share price. If a company has a very high P/E ratio, such as 50 or higher, you should look at it with a very critical eye. It should probably not be near the top of your "buy list" unless you're looking for a very high-growth company, as high-growth companies tend to have higher P/E ratios. Make sure the company has at least some earnings, whether it's $0.10 a share or $2.50 a share, because if it doesn't, chances are it might never reach profitability and can quite possibly end up filing for bankruptcy. The company could also have difficulty raising more capital if they keep talking of a longer-term negative financial outlook.

However, I should point out that many "value" companies that are extremely cheap may have no earnings. These companies can make for good investments, especially if they look like they have positive earnings growth or like they'll be reporting positive earnings in the near future.

You'll also want to evaluate the company's *debt position.* How much *short-term* debt does it have? How much *long-term* debt does it have? If a company keeps piling up short-term debt or long-term debt, it may eventually become buried in debt and never pay it back. That means bankruptcy, as well. In a weak economy, the debt can pile up very fast and companies might not have access to more capital, especially if the stock market is down.

If possible, try to obtain analyst research reports, not for their recommendations, but to see if the analyst mentions the growth potential of the company. Get a feel for what growth will be in the coming quarters and the coming years. You want at least some growth; a company with no growth can be bad—but even a good company can have a bad quarter because of the economy or weak conditions within its industry. In many cases, it can also mean that the company is losing market share in its industry.

Another key point to evaluate is the company's position in its industry. Is it a leader or a laggard? Check the market share of the company—available in analyst research reports and by looking the company up on MultexInvestor. com. Type in a stock symbol and then click on Company

Profile on the left of the screen to see how much of a specific industry's business a company holds.

For example, a larger company operating in the electrical products industry might have 20% of the market, which is a pretty healthy position. In contrast, a company that has less than, say, a 5% market share should be considered a riskier venture, because the company may never be a dominant company in its industry. All large companies start out small and sometimes the biggest opportunity can be found in small stocks, ones with market capitalization under $1 billion. There are considerable opportunities in the small-cap markets, but remember, the risk is higher as well.

It's Your MONEY *The Loser's Game* This term for investing was popularized by Charles D. Ellis, a consultant to institutional investors, who used the term in an article in 1975. He explained that in a loser's game players who try to outdo each other will inevitably fail, while the player who makes fewer mistakes will win the game.

Those are a few of the basics of researching a stock. There are many, many other factors, which include delving into the depths of a company's financial statements, a subject I touched upon, and by reading press releases and research put out by analysts and market research firms. There are other ways to analyze companies. If you don't have the time to do it, try and find an analyst or even a research firm that you like and start following their research to see if anything comes up that's of interest to you.

 Caution *Research Reduces Risk—but Not to Zero* Doing your research is always an important part of investing, but never a sure thing. All investments have some amount of risk.

Stock investing can be profitable, but it can also turn out to be "the loser's game."

Research is not a sure thing, even if you research a company to the fullest extent. Your investment is still at risk, and there are numerous factors—many beyond your control and knowledge—that may reduce the value of your investment.

Researching Bonds

Bonds are fixed-income investments, meaning they provide investors with a steady interest rate. For investment-grade bonds, including government and corporate bonds, the research isn't as extensive as it is for stocks, but we can get help from independent rating agencies like Standard & Poor's and Moody's, as explained in Chapter 6. There are even fixed-income research departments in investment firms, which write reports on the bonds of specific companies, just like equity research departments write reports for stocks.

So, how do we research bonds? The following sections will help you better understand how to do that.

Researching Government Bonds

How does an investor understand government bonds? Look at the countries themselves.

The U.S. is a world superpower. Our country's government-issued bonds are rated AAA by the rating agencies, which is the best rating any country can receive; it means that the odds of the U.S. defaulting on payments to creditors is extremely slim.

The best way to research bonds of other countries is to find out how the rating agencies like Moody's and Standard & Poor's rate those bonds. All of the rating agencies have different criteria and ways of rating the bonds they cover. So, if they all rate a bond high, it's a good sign. To find out more, visit www.moodys.com (select Sovereign) and www.standardand-poors.com (select Fixed Income, then sector: Sovereigns).

If you're going to be researching an emerging market country, then you should really find out everything you need to know about the country's economy as a whole and how healthy it is. Is it on the verge of defaulting on its debt or is it doing well? Find out all of the things there are to know about the country; consult encyclopedias and other resources that provide a wider context for the country's economic situation. There are many resources online that explain this as well, such as the *Central Intelligence Agency World Factbook*, at www.cia.gov. Try to get the reports from Moody's and Standard & Poor's or at least see how they rate the country's debt and the chance of default on the interest payment to creditors.

Since investing in bonds issued by emerging market countries is a very risky practice, I would not recommend this investment for most investors. There is simply too much risk associated with these types of bonds. There are plenty of other choices for you that will allow you to sleep better at night.

Researching Corporate Bonds

When researching a stock, you can get a feel for the company and its business conditions. The same applies to corporate bonds, as the bonds tell much about how the company acts and what it's like. How do you research bonds?

First, you examine the company's financial statements and then get the reports from the rating agencies. This will tell you how safe the company's bonds actually are. Then, you evaluate the company's capital structure, the types of interest rates the bonds are paying, and the maturities. After that, you'll be able to make a more educated decision.

As you may have expected, I'm going to make another plug here for index funds. If you buy individual corporate bonds, you're taking on more risk than if you were to buy a bond index fund. Bond index funds usually aim to trace the performance of the Lehman Brothers Aggregate Bond Index, a benchmark of more than 5,000 bonds that I mentioned in Chapter 3. There are also various other short-, intermediate-, and long-term bond index funds that trace the performance of sections of this index. Just as it's generally better to own stock mutual funds than stocks, it's usually better to own bond mutual funds than bonds. And index funds are the smartest choice.

Researching Municipal Bonds

Researching municipal bonds is almost like researching other types of bonds. However, you have to get the rating agencies' reports and examine what your investment money is being used to finance. There are various types of projects for which municipalities issue bonds—to construct buildings, dams, nuclear power plants, roads, and so forth. Some bonds carry high rates of risk, like for a nuclear power plant, in part because nuclear power is very risky, so they're more likely to pay higher interest rates. The more secure interest rates will come from municipal bonds backed by taxes and other operations, such as the maintenance of sewers and the building of parks and other public places.

Researching High-Yield Bonds

High-yield bonds, as you already know, are extremely risky fixed-income investments that pay higher-than-average interest rates due to the risk they might default. Why are high-yields risky? They're risky because they are issued by untested or distressed companies that may have problems paying back money to creditors or by countries, primarily in the Third World, that may have a tough time competing in the global marketplace and need to struggle to keep the debt from crushing their economy. Usually, though, high-yield bonds, whether they're issued by a company or country, have one thing in common—the company or country has cash flow concerns and can easily become distressed.

But, in many cases high-yield bond funds can be a great diversifier to your portfolio and, if treated with caution and great care, can become a crucial part of your overall asset allocation. While high-yields can be "normal" corporate or government bonds, they have the distinction of more risk. Although there's a lot of risk, there can be a great amount of reward if you stumble upon a winner. Because of this, it's key to cover these in a separate section, because the research process and risk/reward of such bonds can vary greatly from other seemingly "regular" corporate or government bonds.

In Chapter 6 I recommended avoiding investing in high-yield corporate bonds and in Chapter 7 I recommended staying away from high-yield bond funds as well. Consider your risk tolerance; unless you're a gambler, high-yield bonds and funds are probably too risky for your portfolio. However, in some cases you can find opportunities. If you do decide to invest in such bonds as an added diversifier to your portfolio, only do so by way of a high-yield bond index fund or the cheapest possible actively managed high-yield bond fund.

Research and Asset Allocation: A Summary

Asset allocation is very important. You should develop an investment plan and then stick to it. Discipline is key in the investment industry: those who have the most discipline are most likely to be the ones who are ultimately going to succeed. If you keep costs low, keep your portfolio diversified, and have the crucial discipline to stick with your asset allocation plan throughout all market conditions, you're close to reaching the formula for investment success.

Remember: switching in and out of certain investments, just because the market is up or down, is market timing—and most attempts at timing will prove to be harmful to your wealth. Asset allocation is very important to every investor and those who are the most careful will ultimately be better positioned to succeed.

Remember: all the research in the world won't always mean that you'll be a successful investor. There is a misconception put out in the media. The media's equation looks something like: Research = Success. That's just not true. Even with the best of research it's possible for you to lose money. Research helps and by all means you should conduct it. You're likely to make better investment decisions, but you should never forget that picking individual stocks and bonds can still be risky.

The following are the key points from this chapter:

- You should base your asset allocation on your goals, dreams, risk tolerance, and time horizon.
- Researching investments helps a lot, but it won't always

mean you'll earn a return on your investments.

- With seemingly riskier investments, like high-yield bonds, it's wise to consider a mutual fund (specifically, an index fund) rather than individual bonds.

The Path to Wealth: Slowly but Surely Wins the Race

What is the path to wealth and financial success? Slowly building your fortune and then ultimately securing it is the path to investment success. I've already quoted the famed Aesop fable of the tortoise and the hare— "slowly but surely wins the race"—and the moral is especially relevant in the financial markets.

During the Internet heyday of the 1990s, investors were trying anything to make money fast, whether they were day trading, market timing, or throwing large sums of money at the riskiest NAS-DAQ stocks. If you weren't getting rich or at last talking about it, people thought there was something wrong with you! Of course, the fast buck turned out to be more of an illusion, as the NASDAQ lost more than 75% of its value from the high set in March 2000.

Grow rich slowly— you're much more likely to succeed. This chapter explains why.

Trading is not a form of investing. Traders are always buying and selling stocks, trying to figure out the best time to either do one or the other. As such, this is a form of gambling , better left to professionals who do this for a living. If you attempt it, trading can lead to the demise of your wealth, especially if you don't know what you're doing. If you slowly build your wealth, and then you secure it, you'll be successful in the long run.

Building Wealth

You want to build wealth and keep what you make. By owning a diversified portfolio of index funds, you'll be able to increase wealth slowly, but surely. Index funds are traditionally long-term investments. If you have a 20-year time horizon and are hoping to build wealth, index funds will help you achieve your investment objective. As I've discussed, there are a countless number of various index fund allocations.

For example, a young investor with a time horizon of 20 years may want to have an allocation of 80% equity (stock) index funds. In this hypothetical case, the allocation may be 20% domestic mid-cap index fund, 20% domestic small-cap index fund, 20% domestic corporate bond fund, and 40% S&P 500 index fund. This purely hypothetical allocation is aggressive, with 80% in stock indexes, but consistent with a 20-year (possibly even longer) time horizon. This sample portfolio is diversified among different types of stocks, but with only 20% in bonds it will ultimately be dependent upon the stock market for its performance. However, in this case, history is on your side. In a 20-year period, markets have almost always increased in value. As investment guru Charles Ellis puts it in *Winning the Loser's Game,* "The average long-term experience in investing is never surprising, but the short-term experience is always surprising."

A Sample Portfolio for a 20-Year Time Horizon
20% domestic mid-cap index fund
20% domestic small-cap index fund
20% domestic corporate bond fund
40% S&P 500 index fund

Securing Your Wealth

A smart asset allocation and an index fund portfolio that is not overly aggressive will likely build wealth over time. Securing wealth is another story. Once you have realized your investment goals and decide to secure your financial position, you've reached a critical phase in your investment life: you transition from building wealth to securing it.

Whether you choose to invest in bonds for income or mostly equity allocation for growth, there are certain ways to go about securing wealth. The best way to safeguard wealth—keep what you have made—is to buy a short-term bond index fund or a few solid municipal bonds.

Granted, you could simply cash out of all your investments and put it into a bank account, but that's not your best option. The reason: bank accounts traditionally pay low interest rates and inflation may easily exceed the return on your interest. Your return, when adjusted for inflation, will be negative. For example, if you earn 2% in interest and the inflation rate is 3%, you're actually losing money—and that's before taxes are taken into account!

It's better to invest in a group of municipal bonds or a

bond index fund for your needs, because you'll be getting a fixed stream of income and you'll better secure the wealth you have built. In this chapter, you'll be able to better understand the mechanics of building and securing your wealth.

Slowly but Surely: But Why?

Slowly but surely wins the race. But, why? The simplest answer to that question is that people are often too eager to fulfill their investment objectives and trade more often than they should. Inevitably, this leads to attempting to time the market in order to get the greatest returns. As we have learned, trying to get rich quick is hazardous to your wealth. It could over time deplete your ultimate return and eventually leave you broke.

Therefore, the best way to go is "slowly but surely." By increasing your wealth slowly, you'll be able to avoid many of the mistakes made by overly managing your investments, plus you'll be able to sleep better at night not worrying that your investments are going to go south when the markets fall.

Although I've discussed the pluses and minuses of owning some stocks, the best way to build wealth slowly is to be close to 100% indexed in your portfolio at all times (in all types of index funds, both stock and bond), with the possible exception of those close to retirement or retired. Of course, the bond and stock allocations will be vastly different, depending on your age. Vanguard's John Bogle suggests this very simple rule of thumb for figuring the right allocation. Start with your age. If you're 25 years old, that's approximately the right percentage to have in bond funds; the rest, 75%, should be indexed in stock funds, such as an "all market" index fund. It is likely this type of allocation will help you achieve many investment goals you have over your lifetime.

Still, you'll have to make adjustments as your life starts to play out and you reach your goals or change them. By adjusting your allocation, only when needed, you'll be able to weather the ups and downs of the markets and be better positioned to profit as well. It's very hard to maintain your peace of mind during extreme bear markets, at any stage in life. But those who have the discipline to do it and then adjust their asset allocation as needed will be able to survive. One of the many benefits of going slowly but surely is that you don't take unnecessary, uncompensated risk. A slowly-wealth-building portfolio is 100% indexed based on your needs, so you won't take uncompensated risks that could really hurt your return over time.

Losing Your Shirt: You May Not Know It's Happening

Many people want something for nothing, and they think that the stock market is a big slot machine ready to pay a huge jackpot. So they start trading aggressively to boost their returns, which is essentially speculating. Most of these people don't even know what they're doing, and many don't realize there's significantly more risk involved in trading than in index funds and a solid asset allocation. Once investors get into the trading mood, they can lose their shirts. They would have been a lot better off simply indexing their portfolio based on goals and individual needs.

Many people who are losing their shirts investing might not even know why it's happening. The reason? They can't understand the difference between *investing* and *trading*.

To me, if you're making trades daily, weekly, or monthly, that's active trading, and if you're placing trades only every once in a while to correct imbalances in your asset allocations, that's investing. Investing takes discipline and patience and those nonprofessional traders who attempt to beat the market eventually lose their discipline and patience—and might not even know it. Once you start actively trading the markets in search of larger returns, you're making the transition from investor to trader and speculator, which means you're taking many risks. Rational investors never speculate, regardless of market conditions, and therefore do not lose their shirts.

Growing Your Wealth

As I've suggested, it's smart for many investors to have their portfolios 100% indexed and allocated based on needs and goals. Those who can effectively grow their wealth through an asset allocation of index funds will not experience the many fees and expenses that can burden a careless investor's portfolio.

As asset allocations will vary with everyone, it's important that you identify and write down your goals, needs, and wants, and then tailor your asset allocation based on those goals. Asset allocation is not hard and, despite the fact it's not popularized by the media, it's still the best way to go.

Many people carelessly and recklessly invest in anything that sounds promising—without doing any research or taking goals and needs into account. As we saw during the stock market crash of 1929 and the technological boom of the 1990s, people bought any stock, regardless of fundamentals, just because stocks were doing so well and they could make money in anything. That's the wrong way to invest. The people who do that are just hoping their investments pay off, rather than buying based on a sound asset allocation strategy or any other type of plan. Follow the advice of indexing legend John Bogle: "Set an asset allocation of low cost index funds and stay the course." It's as simple as that.

Securing Your Finances

Whether you use bonds or bond index funds while building your wealth, once you achieve your financial goals it's extremely important to secure your wealth. You learned about compound interest in Chapter 4 and the many benefits it offers to all types of investors. There are other alternatives to bonds and the low-interest bearing checking account.

If you put some of your money into a bank certificate of deposit (CD), money market funds, or a related interest-bearing account, you'll be able to grow your wealth while securing it, *even if you're in retirement*. Compound interest provides many benefits to investors and there are thousands of examples of how it pays off for investors. While they won't beat stock market returns or even a bond fund (you don't need to beat the market once you are in the "securing your wealth" phase), CDs and other money market funds can pay off and are a very safe way to invest the money you've made over a lifetime.

Asset allocation is just as important while securing your

finances as it is when growing your finances. While you may no longer want to index your entire portfolio to stock funds, you might want to own bonds or a bond index fund, or you may want to put money into a high-interest-paying bank account so you can use compound interest. Since bonds can provide attractive and healthy interest rates, they make the ideal tool for securing your wealth. Municipal bonds are probably one of the best fixed-income investments for people looking to secure their wealth in a taxable account.

Overall, it's important to realize that securing your wealth is just as important as growing it. After all, what's the point of growing your wealth if you're not able to keep it? As legendary investor Benjamin Graham, author of *The Intelligent Investor*, once said, "There are those who make money in the stock market, and those who keep it."

Staying Financially Fit While Securing Your Wealth

Securing your wealth is crucial, but staying financially fit is even more so. So how do you start staying financially fit? The answer: don't take uncompensated risk in your investments and don't take on too much debt in your personal life.

Because this book is geared toward learning how to invest, I won't spend too much time on personal debt, but it's very important to realize that any debts indirectly affect your investments and will have a long-term detrimental effect on your whole portfolio and your wealth. It all boils down to assets and liabilities. Your assets—investments and your house, cars, etc.—minus your liabilities—house mortgage, car loans, credit card debts, etc.—give you your net worth. If you have too many debts, in the long run it will eat away the return of your investments because the interest payments overshadow your investment gains. This, of course, is bad so you'll want to do anything in your power to reduce liabilities and debts. According to author Michael LeBoeuf, in his book, *The Millionaire in You* (2002): "It's one thing to reach the winner's circle and quite another to stay there. They both take work but of different types. Doing what it takes to stay financially free is job one."

Another hazard to your wealth, as you saw in the previous chapters, is taking uncompensated risk. By that I mean buying individual stocks and risky corporate bonds that you have not researched and do not know much about. If you want to buy individual stocks or bonds, stick to what you know and buy a basket of them. Buy them like you will hold them forever. Overall, don't take any uncompensated risk and don't take on unnecessary debts and liabilities—it's hazardous to your wealth.

> ### *Uncompensated Risk*
>
> "Uncompensated risk" is a technical term in modern portfolio theory, with various meanings. It's basically any risk with which there's no associated return, so it's often a judgment call.
>
> If, for example, you invest in a micro-cap company or in high-yield bonds, the greater risk is compensated by the possibility of a higher return. Is the potential return proportionate to the risk? That's a judgment call. However, if you invest in that stock or those bonds without doing any research, you're gambling that the risk is compensated.

The Path to Wealth: A Summary

For any investor, it's important to understand that growing your wealth is crucial, and so is securing your wealth. Unfortunately, many people fail to realize that they need to secure their wealth and they fall victim to many of the investment fallacies that the media and other sources throw at them. If you stay diversified in index funds during your wealth-building phase and have a good asset allocation, you'll ultimately grow wealth. Once you transition to securing your wealth, it's important to adjust your asset allocation of index funds and not to lose your shirt on foolish strategies like day trading and market timing. Grow your wealth, then secure it and you'll be able to do whatever you want with your life. The following are the two key points from this chapter:

- Invest with the long term in mind, never speculate, and realize that "slowly but surely wins the race."
- Always keep in mind the great advice that Michael LeBoeuf gives in his book, *The Millionaire in You*: "Invest your time actively and your assets passively."

Chapter
14

Put Your Money to Work–Start Saving Now!

When is the best time to save? Now! The answer to that question is always "Now!" because the sooner you start, the sooner you'll be able to grow your wealth. You should always put money on the side by "paying yourself first" every time you get a paycheck. *Consistent* savings is the key. Once you begin to set money aside consistently, you're building your wealth and securing it—a very important part of your overall investment career. This chapter will tell you what types of strategies you can use to put your money away and how and when you should do it.

Don't put off till tomorrow what you can do today— expecially with regard to investing. Here's why.

When You're Not Using Your Money, What Should You Do?

It seems so simple, yet many fail to do it: when you're not using your money, but plan to use it in the near future, what should you do with it? The answer is simple: keep it in an interest-bearing bank account. Not in a shoebox, not in your wallet, not under your mattress, but in something that pays you interest. It's a fact that your worth increases with compound interest and the fact that you're earning money while not using it is very important. People fail to realize that fact and keep a lot of money in their wallets, sometimes even in the form of several hundred-dollar bills. This is the wrong way to store money. Never forget the power of compound interest and its power for building wealth.

Surprisingly, your money is at risk when it's sitting in your wallet and *not* in the bank. Is the threat from criminals? Well, yes, that's also a possibility. But more importantly, it's threatened by inflation. As we discussed earlier, inflation erodes your wealth. The reason? Inflation is the upward movement of goods and services that make up our economy, and the value of the dollar decreases because people can't buy as much with their money. Inflation will eat away at the value of your money as it sits in your wallet or a shoebox, especially if you keep it there for a few years. Yes, it's surprising but people keep money in such places and fail to realize the benefits of com-

It's Your MONEY — Park Your Money

Investment professionals talk about *parking* money. This simply means putting it somewhere when you're not ready to invest it yet. Not just any "somewhere," of course— but in interest-bearing accounts such as savings or money market funds where it's easily accessible when the time comes to invest it.

pound interest. Keep your spare money in the bank at all times (if possible) so you can earn interest.

Why It's Important to Start Saving and Investing Now

You need to start saving your money now—you don't have a day to lose. Every day counts. Think of it this way: every day that goes by, you "give away" some money because you're failing to recognize the importance of saving your money and accumulating interest. If you save your money so it can earn interest in a bank account or a fixed-income investment or any other type of investment, you'll be in a lot better position in the long run. Time is money: the more time you have to invest, the more money you can make. It's a lot easier to make $1 million in 50 years than to make $1 million in one year. That's what's meant by the phrase "time is money."

Whenever you have the chance to put away any amount of money, whether it's $1 or $1,000, you should do it. For example, if you put $1,000 in the bank at an interest rate of 4% for a year and don't contribute any other money to it, your ending amount would be $1,040. While that may not be a lot, it all adds up. I've made a lot of money simply through saving it whenever I can. Compound interest and even simple interest—as in the example of the $1,000—are great tools because you can make money with money, without having to do anything! The faster you put your money away and devote it to some sort of investment, whether it's an index fund or a bank account, the sooner you will start building your wealth.

A common question is "How does the bank make money if they're paying you interest?" The answer is the bank loans your money to other people, who pay the bank a higher rate than it pays you. Therefore, it is making money from the *spread* between interest earned and interest paid. This system helps you build wealth, it helps the person who needs money get a loan, and it helps the people at the bank earn a living. Banking is a "win, win, win" situation.

Ultimately, if you invest now, your wealth will be greater in the future. It's simple: the sooner you start to invest your money, the more time you have for your investments to make gains for you. As the title of this section suggests,

 **Spread** The spread in banking is the percentage difference between the interest rates the bank charges on loans and the interest rates the bank pays on deposits.

investing now definitely translates into greater returns in the future. The longer time you have, the longer time you are allowing your investment to appreciate and grow. Anyway you look at it, investing and saving now will ultimately translate into higher gains. Capitalize on the world's most precious commodity—time.

Risk, Reward, and Saving Money

When you put money away into a bank account, is there a chance that you will lose your money and have your total deposit wiped out? No—unless you've got more than $100,000 in that bank. As explained in Chapter 4, the Federal Deposit Insurance Corporation (FDIC) insures all deposits made in legal U.S. banks up to $100,000 per individual; anything over that amount is not insured. If the bank goes bankrupt and you have more than $100,000 in any accounts there, there might be a chance you can lose some or even all of your money. So it's best to only have $100,000 in any bank.

Whether it's the U.S. government or an investment firm, nobody likes to see a bankrupt bank. That's not good for the people who lost money or for the public's confidence in the banking industry.

The risk/reward equation in a bank account is simple: little risk, little reward. But I don't like to think of it like that; after all, why would I be such a big advocate of compound interest if the reward was so little? The reward is great, because the money keeps building up. Every day the money you have in the bank grows, whether it's by a few cents or a few dollars, and even though it may seem small, it can really add up.

Put Your Money to Work—Start Saving Now: A Summary

Overall, it's important to start saving right now. The sooner you save and put the money away, either in a bank, an index fund, or some other investment instrument, you'll at least put yourself on the path to investment success. Of course, you need a good asset allocation plan. Time equals money and vice versa. The longer the time you have to invest, the more money you will make. You can easily make a lot of money over many years if you invest right, as opposed to a lot of money in one or a few years. The more you save, the more you'll be able to invest and, especially if you build a portfolio of index funds tailored to your specific needs, you'll likely achieve your investment goals. The following are key points from this chapter:

- Start saving as early as possible and try to earn the highest interest possible on your money wherever you may put it.
- Remember that time is one of your greatest assets, particularly when you're young.
- Don't put more than $100,000 in any one bank account, since that is all the FDIC will insure.

Chapter
15

Navigating Rough Markets: Safe Havens for Nervous Investors

Are you a perpetual worrier? Or are you just nervous when the markets go down? If you're either of those, chances are you'll want at least some of your money to be invested in a safe haven when the going gets rough. This chapter will help you understand the safe havens in the markets and where you can invest if you find yourself worrying too much about the financial markets.

It's worth noting that you can't avoid all risk. Nothing is 100% for sure. Once you take away all risk, you take away all potential reward; therefore, you're left with nothing after taxes and inflation. So, if you want a return with minimal risk during tough market conditions, then this chapter will help you realize there are opportunities even in tough markets—you just need to know where to look.

Sometimes the stock market gets a little weird and scary. Here are some alternative investments for you to consider.

A Misconception: You Can Diversify Away All of Your Risk

If a broker or planner ever tries to tell that you can earn maximum returns with no risk, look for a new advisor. A common misconception that the media throws at investors is that they can diversify all of their risk and still earn high returns. That is completely wrong and the people who are spreading such lies probably have no idea what they're talking about.

While I'm a huge fan of diversification, I've got to warn you against believing this common fallacy that all risk can be diversified away while still earning high returns—it's just not possible. Even a portfolio solely invested in U.S. government bonds carries *interest rate risk*. That's the possibility that changes in interest rates will decrease the value of an investment. So, if interest rates rise while you're holding bonds, the value of your bonds falls. The longer the term of the bond, the more the value falls. Your bond may be totally safe, "backed by the full faith and credit of the U.S. government," but it's still losing value.

Interest rate risk

Interest rate risk is the possibility that changes in interest rates will decrease the value of an investment. It is primarily a problem with fixed-income investments, such as bonds: as interest rates rise, the prices of bonds drop.

There's always some type of risk apparent in the financial markets. If there were no risk, there would be no reward. Even a well-diversified portfolio, one with investments spread over various asset classes, still carries risk. There might be less risk because of diversification, but there's still risk involved. Remember: you can't diversify away all aspects of risk when investing.

Do you remember Harry Markowitz from Chapter 4, the "father" of modern portfolio theory (MPT)? He stated that investors would reduce their risk by spreading their money across various asset classes.

That may seem simplistic. If so, then here's a brief but more sophisticated explanation. MPT considers a number of investments and explores the possibilities for optimal portfolios based on those investments. If we know the expected returns, the volatilities (risks), and the *correlations* among those investments, we can calculate the expected return and volatility of any portfolio that can be built from those investments. The set of optimal portfolios that results is called the *efficient frontier*. I could go into detail, but it would take too long and be more involved than necessary to make my basic point here—diversification.

I would recommend to many investors that following MPT is one of the better investment ideas around. You should spread your money over various asset classes to

It's Your MONEY **Correlation** A correlation or a *correlation coefficient* is a measure of the tendency of two investments to move in the same direction or opposite directions. If two investments tend to move in the same direction at the same time, the correlation is *positive*. If two investments tend to move in opposite directions at the same time, the correlation is *negative*. If two investments tend to move independently of each other, then there's no correlation. A correlation coefficient of 1.0 is the worst: the two investments provide no diversification at all. A correlation coefficient of –1.0 would be ideal for diversification.

reduce risk and enhance returns. In terms of correlations, this would mean mixing asset classes that do not have a high positive correlation. That could be—at a very basic level—stocks and bonds or it could be U.S. stocks and foreign stocks or large-cap stocks and small-cap stocks. If you're into numbers, you could consult tables of correlation coefficients to take your asset allocation to a higher level.

Real Estate

One investment we have not yet discussed is real estate.

Hard asset In investing, any of a wide range of physical commodities, such as real estate, precious metals, precious stones, antiques, coins, works of art, and "collectibles."

Real estate has been a safe haven for investors in rough economic times, when the stock market has been down. Why is real estate so special? Unlike stocks and mutual funds, real estate is a *hard* asset—a physical property that people can use, something real.

REITs

If you're an investor, you can buy an actual piece of real estate or you can buy a portfolio of real estate in a real estate investment trust (REIT), as explained in Chapter 7. So, how would buying a physical piece of property hedge you against certain risks that you might experience during hard times, when the stock market is riskier? The answer is fairly simple: during bad economic times, interest rates tend to fall. This causes property owners to be able to refinance mortgages. When doing so, they're paying back at a lower interest rate, and it leaves more room for profit for the REITs. Second, REITs can be a good hedge (especially when diversified among the various classes of property, like office and healthcare-related REITs) because they own and invest in physical property. This property is essential to our economy and our lives, so even in bad economic conditions, property owners will continue paying mortgages off. REITs that invest in or own healthcare properties (such as hospitals and nursing homes), apartment complexes, and other properties will do well, because people will continue to need healthcare and places to live, whatever the economic conditions.

Thus, some forms of real estate can be an effective hedge against downturns in the economy. However, such forms of real estate as office property and hotels can be ineffective in a bad economy. That's because the companies that occupy the offices may be suffering and, in some cases, may leave the property, which means less rent coming to the property owners. Hotel properties suffer because people tend to travel less when times are bad, which causes a decline in income for the hotels and the REITs that have invested in them.

Aside from their own homes, people are rarely going to want to buy a hard asset such as other real estate properties because of the large amounts of money and the extensive paperwork involved. So they might stick to the companies that do it for them (REITs). There are various types of REITs, which invest in various types of real estate such as office, retail, hotel and motel, apartments, and other properties. A REIT is like a mutual fund of real estate that gets their money from the rent on buildings they lease to tenants. You simply buy shares in the REIT, which owns real estate, so you don't have to actually buy or manage the physical properties. REITs also usually pay an attractive dividend, which can be nice during a downtrend when some other companies might cut back on their dividends. In addition, REITs are liquid, unlike real estate. REITs can be an essential part of your portfolio and can even make for attractive investments in bull markets. But one word of caution: REIT's can drop in value when the overall markets tank. Rather than buying individual REITs, an investor can look no further than a REIT index fund, such as the Vanguard REIT Index (VGSIX), which is convenient and provides diversification.

REIT Funds: Actively Managed and Index Funds

For those not wishing to venture into buying individual REITs or real estate-related companies, you might be interested in REIT and real estate funds, whether they're actively managed or passively managed. A passively managed, REIT index fund may track the Morgan Stanley REIT Index, made up of more than 100 REITs. But there are other indexes as well. There are also various actively managed REIT funds, though the expenses, as with most actively managed funds, are higher than with an index fund.

One of the other benefits of REIT funds is that they tend to pay high dividends—offering attractive yields to investors. REITs usually generate a nice amount of cash quarter to quarter and pay it to shareholders in the form of dividends. The shareholders of REIT funds get to share in the excitement, because they too get those dividends. In fact, REITs are required to pay out most of their earnings to shareholders.

There are various REIT actively managed counterparts, though, as in most actively managed funds, the expenses are higher than an index fund. You might want to consider owning the Vanguard REIT Index (VGSIX) as a good all-around index fund.

If you do want to go with a REIT fund that attempts to beat the market, which one do you choose? A good way to do that is to go onto Morningstar.com and search for "REIT." Examine the specific REIT funds listed, and check their holdings. (REIT funds must have at least 80% of their assets invested in REITs or REIT-related issues.) If there are any of interest, request some literature from the fund company and read and learn more about the fund. See what expense ratio the fund charges and whether or not it's worth investing in or if it's simply better to go with a REIT index fund.

A question that might come up now is "Should REITs be a regular part of my asset allocation?" My answer is "Yes." Because I advocate a 100% indexed portfolio, you can buy a REIT index fund, such as the Vanguard REIT Index Fund (VGSIX) and devote about 5%-10% of your total asset allocation to the fund, as an added diversifier. In addition to bonds, this will likely add further safety to most portfolios.

Real Estate, REITs, and REIT Funds: A Summary

I hope that, after reading the section on real estate, REITs, and REIT funds, you feel more comfortable with the subject. REITs and real estate can be great hedging tools and I highly recommend them. Ralph Block, author of *Investing in REITS: Real Estate Investment Trusts*, says, "REITs' high current yield often act as a shock absorber against daily market fluctuations." A REIT provides an attractive yield, which is great in and of itself because it's a guaranteed return—that is, of course, unless the REIT decides to stop paying dividends.

I highly recommend purchasing a REIT index fund as a hedge for your portfolio. Many people can't stomach the volatility that the market provides and therefore look for safe havens to park their money. REITs can provide some of that protection: you just need to do a little homework to find out what's right for you.

Gold and Other Precious Metals

Gold and other precious metals can provide an even better hedge than real estate against market downturns, economic and political upheaval, and the much-despised inflation. Gold and other precious metals have been purchased for thousands of years for their beauty, but also for their safety in times of turmoil. Many people store gold to have a sense of security and to help them sleep better at night. There are even whole books written on how you can profit from gold and other precious metals.

 **Precious metals** In investing, precious metals are gold, silver, platinum, and palladium. These metals may be traded either physically (e.g., bars or coins) or through futures and options contracts, stocks and bonds of mining companies, mutual funds, or other investment instruments.

While precious metals will provide a small return, history has proven that they simply keep pace with inflation over time, and that's all. If you live in the U.S. and are afraid of a war involving our country, gold may provide you with peace of mind and comfort in case the worst does in fact happen. While I don't advocate stocking up on gold bars and other precious metals, I do believe that people can occasionally find an opportunity in a mutual fund that invests in gold and other precious metals.

Gold

In this section, you'll get to better understand gold the metal, gold companies, gold mutual funds and you'll be able to determine whether or not these investments should be a part of your asset allocation.

If you're looking for some sort of return, don't waste your money on gold bars; they do not generate any dividends or income. It's better to concentrate on gold-related mutual funds, rather than coins and bars.

Investors also invest in companies that are involved in mining, refining, and selling gold. Many companies are very risky and provide an extreme amount of uncompensated risk. Why? Because many gold mining companies fail to locate enough gold for the company to make a business out of it. Unless you're actually in the gold mines and see gold being produced, I would recommend staying away from such investments.

In my opinion, if you want to own gold, it's best to do it with a mutual fund. That way, you diversify your risk among hundreds of companies, both large and small.

Silver

Silver—"the other precious metal," as some call it—is also a hedge against political upheaval, but not to the extent of gold. I wouldn't recommend buying bars of silver even if there were economic or political turmoil in the United States. Silver is the most plentiful and least expensive of the precious metals. It's currently valued at a little less than $5 an ounce. If you bought silver bars or coins, you would have to buy a gigantic safe to store them! If you're looking to own silver, I recommend doing it through a precious metals mutual fund. Like gold mining companies, most silver mining companies are extremely risky and are considered speculations due to the fact that some may never pay off. Remember: Wall Street is full of false promises and some gold and silver companies are just that. In my opinion, silver companies can be extremely hazardous to an investor's wealth.

I advise you not to take the huge uncompensated risks that individual company shares pose and the huge burden they may put on your portfolio. Rather, concentrate on diversification with a precious metals mutual fund.

Precious Metals Funds

There's no broad-based precious metals index fund. So, if you want to buy a precious metal mutual fund, you should look at actively managed precious metals funds. There are plenty of them; to take a look at them, visit Mornignstar.com and search for "precious metals" or, if you're just looking for an actively managed gold fund, search for "gold." There are many fund companies offering precious metals funds; if you decide to seriously consider adding them to your portfolio, be sure to check the expense ratio and be sure to request literature from the fund company.

Precious Metals and Asset Allocation

Should precious metals be a part of your asset allocation? My answer is no. There are too many variables, and odds are they won't pay off as investments. What about gold and silver mining shares? They are way too risky and present a huge uncompensated risk. Should a precious metals or gold mutual fund be a part of an investor's asset allocation? Maybe, but don't bet the house on it.

If you want a safe haven, turn to a REIT index fund instead, as discussed in the previous section. Precious metals funds may be safe havens in political turmoil, but usually don't pay dividends as high as REIT funds. Many small gold and silver mining firms may never pay dividends and, unlike REITs, have no "shock absorber" in times of market volatility. All in all, I would highly advise you not to bother with any aspect of precious metals at all. If history offers even an inkling of what the future may bring, it doesn't appear that you'll need precious metals anytime soon.

The Best Diversifier: Bonds

The subject of the last section of this chapter has been explained in depth in previous chapters, particularly Chapters 6 and 12. Bonds or fixed-income investments are safe havens for investors in times of market downturns and a weak economy. Bonds are great diversifiers in a portfolio, especially due to the fact they provide the investor with a stream of income regardless of what the economy is doing or where the market is headed. That holds true for almost every bond, except high-yield bonds. If you stick with high-quality bonds and avoid high-yield bonds, then you'll most likely be safe when you most need that sense of security.

Why Bonds Are Not Only Safe Havens, but Essential

Bonds are safe havens because they provide investors with a fixed stream of income. But they're not only safe havens—they're essential to *any* investor's portfolio. Regardless of age or any other factor, investors need at least some bonds in their portfolios. Whether they come in the form of a bond fund or a bond index fund—they belong in every investor's portfolio. Your total allocation should have some combination of stocks and bonds. What percentage should you invest in stocks and what percentage in bonds? That's the most important decision you will make, and you should decide, perhaps with the help and guidance of a broker or a planner.

Your exact allocations should be based on your risk tolerance, age, needs, wants and of course, goals. A fixed stream of income is always nice, regardless of what the market is doing. It's nice to know that money is coming in, even in the harshest of times. A nice amount for a young investor would be 15%-20% in bonds, but for older investors the percentage increases with age because they do not need to take as much risk anymore.

But what types of bonds make for good investments? I would buy municipal bonds or municipal bond funds in taxable accounts, as they are a great added diversifier for investors looking to add bonds to their portfolio.

Remember: you should always have a portion of your money invested in bonds and/or bond index funds. When the market is not performing well, bonds tend to perform well and therefore will likely compensate you for the stocks that are going down and also compensate you for the greater risk you're taking when investing in individual stocks and stock funds.

Those looking for a bond index fund should look no further than the Vanguard Total Bond Market Index (VBMFX), which owns the bonds in the Lehman Brothers Aggregate Bond Index, a benchmark of more than 5,000 bonds. The Vanguard Total Bond Market Index is a cheap and effective way to own the whole bond market.

It's Your MONEY

Bonds and Your Portfolio

Bonds should be a part of every investor's portfolio—but the allocation depends on age and risk tolerance.

Overall, bonds are a safe haven during rough times. They provide income and make for an essential part of your asset allocation, no matter how old you are.

Navigating Rough Markets: A Summary

Overall, you need some protection during rough markets and when the economy is sour; I believe that you should devote some of your asset allocation to a REIT index fund and to bonds. When things get rough, don't intentionally increase the positions of your hedges—that's market timing. Don't jump in and out of investments. Adjust your portfolio only at fixed times, say, the end or beginning of the year. You should do this to adjust your asset allocation back to its target balance.

Don't bother with gold and other precious metals. They do not pay interest or dividends and only keep up with inflation in the long run.

When there are rough markets and sour economic conditions, don't get nervous or scared. The U.S. economy has always prevailed. If you're in international markets, they might be causing some of your nervousness, so allocate your money according to your risk tolerance.

Remember: slow and steady wins the race. As John Bogle, the legendary founder of the Vanguard Group, always says, "Stay the course." If you stay the course, in the end you'll be fine.

The following are the key points from this chapter:

- You should realize that there are many safe havens for you in tough markets, including bonds and REITs.
- Stay away from direct investments in gold, silver, and individual mining stocks. They do not generate enough returns for the risk.

- Make sure that at least a portion of your portfolio is devoted to bonds.
- These types of safe havens might be a part of your asset allocation, but *never* switch in and out of the specific asset classes. That's market timing—and it's hazardous to your wealth.

Index

Nations Managed Index Fund
(NMIMX), index funds, 112
NAV (net asset value), 84–85
Net asset value (NAV), 84–85
New York Stock Exchange (NYSE),
10, 16
Newsletters, advice, 6
NMIMX (Nations Managed Index
Fund), index funds, 112
No-penalty CDs, 28
North American Securities
Administrators Association, 37
Notes, 78
NYSE (New York Stock Exchange),
10, 16

O

Odd lot, 127
Odd-lot differential, 127
Over-the-counter (OTC) stocks, 16
Overlap, index funds, 110–111
"Owning the market," index funds,
110

P

P/E (price-to-earnings ratio),
65–66
Paine Webber Enhanced NAS-
DAQ 100 Index Fund (PWNAX),
index funds, 112
Parking money, 174
Passive management *versus* active
management, 86–89
PEP (PepsiCo), 22
PepsiCo (PEP), 22
Peterson, Pamela P., *Analysis of
Financial Statements*, 153
Plans, 40–41
cash, 44–45
diversification, 43–44
goals, 42–43
monthly savings, 45–46
timelines, 41–42

Precious metals
alternative investments, 186
asset allocation, 188–189
funds, 188
Preferred stocks, 10
Price-to-earnings ratio (P/E), 65–66
company research, 154
Prices, stocks, 3
Prospectus, mutual funds, 98
Publications
Analysis of Financial Statements,
153
Beating the Street, 6
Intelligent Investor, The, 170
*Interpretation of Financial
Statements, The*, 153
Keys to Reading an Annual Report,
153
Millionaire in You, The, 171
Wall Street Journal, The, 13
Pump and dump, 120
PWNAX (Paine Webber Enhanced
NASDAQ 100 Index Fund),
index funds, 112

R

Ratings
bonds, 76–77
research, 67
Real estate
REIT funds, 184–185
REITs, 182–184
Real estate investment trust
(REIT) funds, 95–96
Regular investors, 52
REIT funds (real estate investment
trust funds), 95–96, 184–185
REITs (real estate investment
trust), 182–184
Reports, research, 67
Research, 4–8, 143–145, 150–151
bonds, 157–161

About the Author

Timothy Olsen is a 14 year old investor who has been investing and researching the financial markets since the age of 8. He has been featured in a variety of sources including REITStreet and CNBC. He has written articles and done research for SageTrade.com and Morningstar.com (among others) and is working on contributing articles to IndexFunds.com. In the future, he wants to pursue a career in the financial services industry and hopes to become a fee only advisor, analyst, or hedge fund manager.